HOTSPOTS

CYPRUS

Written by George McDonald; updated by Kathryn Liston

Published by Thomas Cook Publishing
A division of Thomas Cook Tour Operations Limited.
Company registration no. 1450464 England
The Thomas Cook Business Park, Unit 9, Coningsby Road,
Peterborough PE3 8SB, United Kingdom
Email: books@thomascook.com, Tel: + 44 (0)1733 416477
www.thomascookpublishing.com

Produced by Cambridge Publishing Management Limited
Burr Elm Court, Main Street, Caldecote CB23 7NU

ISBN: 978-1-84157-975-7

Project Editor: Karen Fitzpatrick
Production/DTP: Steven Collins

Printed and bound in Spain by GraphyCems

CONTENTS

WHAT'S IN YOUR GUIDEBOOK?

Independent authors Impartial, up-to-date information from our travel experts who meticulously source local knowledge.

Experience Thomas Cook's 165 years in the travel industry and guidebook publishing enriches every word with expertise you can trust.

Travel know-how Contributions by thousands of staff around the globe, each one living and breathing travel.

Editors Travel-publishing professionals, pulling everything together to craft a perfect blend of words, pictures, maps and design.

You, the traveller We deliver a practical, no-nonsense approach to information, geared to how you really use it.

Pafos harbour area

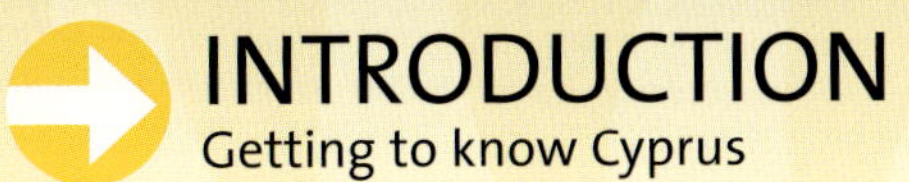

INTRODUCTION
Getting to know Cyprus

Cyprus
0
10 km
0
5 miles
...Limit of area under Turkish occupation
...City
...Large Town
...Small Town
...POI
...Motorway
...Main Road
...Minor Road
...Airport
N
Cape Kormakitis
Livera
Karava
Myrtou
Morfou Bay
Skylloura
Morfou
Pentageia
Pomos
Karavostasi
Cape Arnaoutis
Akaki
Peristerona
Argaka
Latsi
Polis
B9
Neo Chorio
Kakopetria
Troodos
Olympus
1951
CYPRUS
Mountains
Giolou
Agros
Pegeia
E709
Coral Bay
Episkopi
Pachna
Pafos
Geroskipou
Timi
Agios Amvrosios
Acheleia
Kouklia
A1
Pafos
A6
Episkopi
LEMESOS
Pissouri
Episkopi Bay
Salt Lake
Akrotiri
Cape Gata
Turkey
Greece
Cyprus

Cape Apostolos Andreas
Karpasia
Rizokarpason
Aigialousa
Galiniporni
Davlos
Galateia
Koma tou Gialou
Keryneia
Kalograia
Agios Theodoros
Klepini
Range
Bogazi
Pentadaktylos
Lefkonoiko
UNDER TURKISH OCCUPATION SINCE 1974
Ammochostos Bay
LEFKOSIA
Agios Seryios
cosia
Strovolos
Ammochostos
Famagusta
Lysi
Deryneia
A1
Pera Chorio
Ormideia
Agia Napa
Protaras
Kochi
A2
A3
Xylofagou
Cape Gkreko
Stavrovouni
Nissi Beach
Harbour
Larnaka
A1
A5
efkara
Larnaka
Larnaka Bay
Kiti
Kofinou
Cape Kiti
Mazotos
Zygi
Mediterranean Sea

Getting to know Cyprus

Cyprus is a Mediterranean holiday island *par excellence* that extends a warm welcome to visitors and has much to offer. Sunshine, blue skies, beaches, vineyards, orange and lemon groves, a multicoloured carpet of flowers in spring, wild mountain ranges, cedar forests and remote villages are all to be discovered on this beautiful island.

APHRODITE'S ISLAND

In Greek mythology, Aphrodite, the goddess of love, was born here, drifting ashore on a seashell. As the Homeric Hymn to Aphrodite tells it:

I will sing of stately Aphrodite, gold-crowned and beautiful,
Whose dominion is the walled cities of all sea-set Cyprus.
There the moist breath of the West Wind wafted her over the waves of the loud-moaning sea.

Cypriots have taken Aphrodite to their hearts, and who can blame them?

HISTORY

Stone Age tombs, Greek temples, Roman mosaics, Byzantine monasteries, Crusader castles, Gothic abbeys, Arab mosques, Turkish bath-houses, Imperial British hill stations – where else but Cyprus? The island has always been a crossroads and visiting civilisations left the signature of their passing in many ruined historic sites.

CLIMATE

With around 3,000 hours of sunshine annually, Cyprus is well acquainted with that golden ball in the sky. From spring through to autumn, good weather is pretty well guaranteed, with summer temperatures soaring into the 30s°C (90s°F). Spring and autumn are milder, with the possibility of rain. Even in winter, the climate can be warm, although mixed with periods of rain, and even snow in the Troodos Mountains. If you find yourself caught in a rainstorm, you can take comfort from the fact that the island badly needs the water to restore reservoirs and underground supplies that have been depleted by drought.

BEACHES

Cyprus has good if not very extensive beaches around Agia Napa, Protaras, Larnaka, Lemesos and Pafos, and at points in between. There are also tiny beaches in the rugged Akamas Peninsula, and some very quiet ones along the north coast east of Polis. Most of the popular beaches have a range of services that may include lounger and umbrella hire, beach cafés and restaurants, pedalos, and watersports facilities.

Remember to take safety seriously on the beach and in the sea, especially with young children – calm as the seas around Cyprus look, they are subject to very strong currents. And be careful not to overdo the sunbathing, particularly at the beginning of your holiday, and once again particularly with children.

GEOGRAPHY

Lefkosia is the capital, and lies in the middle of the island, at the heart of the agricultural Mesaoria Plain. Just as Cyprus is a divided island at present, Lefkosia is a divided capital. The Cyprus army is on one side of the Green Line, facing Turkish occupation troops on the other side, with United Nations peacekeepers in the middle. Notable places in the Turkish-occupied area are the Pentadaktylos Mountains, the resort of Keryneia (Kyrenia) and the once opulent medieval city of Ammochostos (Famagusta).

The south-coast resorts around Agia Napa and Protaras offer an escape that many sun-starved north Europeans dream of, while Larnaka and Lemesos act as both important business centres and holiday resorts. In the west, Pafos is another important resort area. North of Pafos, the small resorts of Polis and Latsi lie between the Akamas Peninsula wilderness to the west and the relatively untouched northeast coast.

A little way inland from the coast, you enter a different Cyprus, a place of timeless villages and rugged scenery, reaching up to the windy heights of the Troodos Mountains, and the 1,952-m (6,404-ft) summit of Mount Olympus. There are Byzantine monasteries and churches, tranquil villages and hard-working farmers who produce a cornucopia of fruits, vegetables and grapes for wine.

THE BEST OF CYPRUS

Cyprus has a wide range of fascinating places to see and visit. Many of them are either archaeological or religious in nature, reflecting the island's long and colourful history.

TOP 10 ATTRACTIONS

- **Choirokoitia Neolithic Village** The foundations of circular homes occupy a bleak hillside near Larnaka. They were occupied from the 7th to the 4th centuries BC by Stone Age people who buried their dead under the floors (see page 71).

- **Cyprus Archaeological Museum** Lefkosia's top museum houses a superb historical collection, including the Aphrodite of Soli and a bronze statue of Roman Emperor Septimius Severus (see page 17).

- **Hala Sultan Tekke** This notable mosque stands on the shore of Larnaka's Salt Lake, and incorporates the tomb of Hala Sultan, a relative of the Prophet Mohammed who died in Cyprus in AD 649 (see pages 38 and 72).

- **Kolossi Castle** This castle near Lemesos was the Grand Commandery of the Knights of the Order of St John of Jerusalem, and later of the Knights Templar, after the Crusaders were driven out of the Holy Land in 1291 (see page 75).

- **Larnaka Fort** Larnaka Fort was built in 1625, and occupies a dramatic position overlooking the sea (see page 39).
- **Mount Olympus** The highest peak of the Troodos range, Mount Olympus reaches 1,952 m (6,404 ft). In winter you can ski there (see page 85).
- **Omodos** This is a restored village that lies in the foothills of the Troodos Mountains, where several arts and crafts workshops have been established and residents invite visitors for guided tours of their traditional homes (see page 89).
- **Rock of Aphrodite** An unusual rock formation in the sea beside the Lemesos–Pafos road. This is the legendary spot where Aphrodite, the Greek goddess of love, was born and was washed ashore on a seashell (see page 80).
- **Stavrovouni Monastery** Stavrovouni perches on top of a 610-m (2,000-ft) rocky outcrop with a view over the desolate landscape between Lefkosia and Larnaka. St Helena founded the monastery in AD 327 (see page 66).
- **Tombs of the Kings** Dating from the 3rd century BC to the 3rd century AD, this is a complex of rock-cut tombs beside the sea, in which leading citizens of Pafos were buried (see page 56).

Rock of Aphrodite, Pafos

SYMBOLS KEY

The following symbols are used throughout this book:

address telephone fax website address email
opening times important

The following symbols are used on the maps:

information office
post office
shopping
airport
hospital
police station
bus station
church
city
large town
small town
POI (point of interest)
motorway
main road
minor road
mosque
numbers denote featured cafés, restaurants & evening venues

RESTAURANT CATEGORIES

The symbol after the name of each restaurant listed in this guide indicates the price of a typical main course plus starter or dessert and drink for one person.

£ = under £7 **££** = £7–£15 **£££** = over £15

One of Cyprus' attractive harbours

RESORTS
Places under the sun

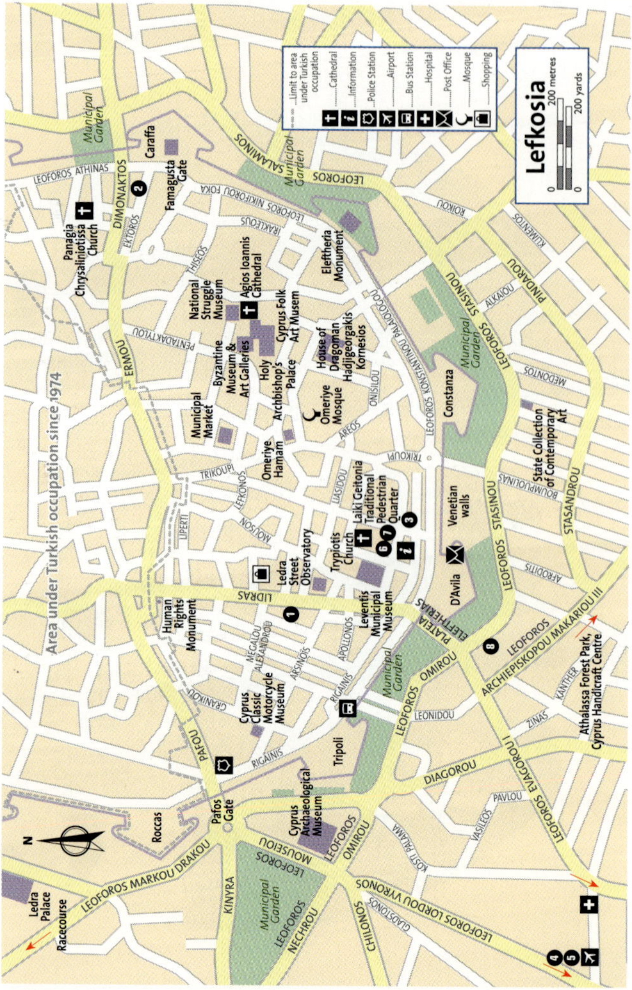

Lefkosia

0 200 metres
0 200 yards

Limit to area under Turkish occupation
Cathedral
Information
Police Station
Airport
Bus Station
Hospital
Post Office
Mosque
Shopping

Area under Turkish occupation since 1974

Ledra Palace
Racecourse
Roccas
Pafos Gate
Cyprus Archaeological Museum
Tripoli
Cyprus Classic Motorcycle Museum
Human Rights Monument
Ledra Street Observatory
Leventis Municipal Museum
Trypiotis Church
Laiki Geitonia Traditional Pedestrian Quarter
D'Avila
Venetian walls
Constanza
Municipal Market
Omeriye Hamam
Omeriye Mosque
Byzantine Museum & Art Galleries
Holy Archbishop's Palace
House of Dragoman Hadjigeorgakis Kornesios
Cyprus Folk Art Musem
National Struggle Museum
Agios Ioannis Cathedral
Eleftheria Monument
Panagia Chrysaliniotissa Church
Famagusta Gate
Caraffa
State Collection of Contemporary Art
Municipal Garden
Athalassa Forest Park, Cyprus Handicraft Centre

LEOFOROS MARKOU DRAKOU
KINYRA
LEOFOROS NECHROU
CHILONOS
LEOFOROS MOUSEIOU
LEOFOROS OMIROU
LEOFOROS LORDOU VYRONOS
GLADSTONOS
KOSTI PALAMA
VASILEOS
PAVLOU
DIAGOROU
LEOFOROS EVAGOROU I
ZINAS
KANTHER
LEONIDOU
LEOFOROS ARCHIEPISKOPOU MAKARIOU III
PLATEIA ELEFTHERIAS
AFRODITIS
STASANDROU
LEOFOROS STASINOU
BOUMPOULINAS
MEDONTOS
PINDAROU
ALKAIOU
KIMENTOS
ROIKOU
LEOFOROS SALAMINOS
LEOFOROS KONSTANTINOU PALAIOLOGOU
TRIKOUPI
AREOS
ONISILOU
LEOFOROS NIKIFOROU FOKA
IRAKLEOUS
THISEOS
PENTADAKTYLOU
ERMOU
DIMONAKTOS
EKTOROS
LEOFOROS ATHINAS
PAFOU
RIGAINIS
GRANIKOU
ARSINOIS
MEGALOU ALEXANDROU
APOLLONOS
LIDRAS
LIPERTI
LEFKONOS
MOUSON
SASIDOU

Lefkosia (Nicosia)

The city of Lefkosia (Nicosia) is a modern and sophisticated capital. At its heart is Old Lefkosia, scarred by the 'Green Line' that separates the south from the Turkish-controlled north. Political events relating to the Cyprus problem and the EU accession have resulted in the partial opening of checkpoints to Cypriots as well as to tourists from abroad who choose to make the day's visit to the other side.

At the same time, the inner city is, in places, a glorious evocation of times past, with its crumbling – and now increasingly restored – mud-brick and sandstone houses. These are jumbled in with mosques from whose minarets the faithful are summoned to prayer, Orthodox churches glimmering with lamps and icons, and Ottoman baths, inns

The statue of Makarios at the Archbishop's Palace

GUIDED TOURS
Walking tours are offered free of charge by the Lefkosia Municipality. They include: Walking Tour of Lefkosia (Thursdays); Chrysaliniotissa and Kaimakli – The Past Restored (Mondays); Lefkosia – Outside the Walls (Fridays). Tours in English depart 10.00 from the Cyprus Tourist Organisation office and take two hours.
ⓐ 11 Aristokyprou Street, Laiki Gitonia ⓣ 22 67 42 64

and villas. For information, visit Lefkosia's tourist information office at 11 Aristokyprou Street, Laiki Geitonia ⓣ 22 67 42 64

THINGS TO SEE & DO

Agios Ioannis Cathedral (St John's Cathedral)

Lefkosia's splendid little Orthodox cathedral stands beside the Archbishop's Palace. Built in 1662, it has an abundance of murals and icons, with gilt decoration and sparkling coloured lamps. The pulpit is graced with a magnificent double-headed eagle, the emblem of Byzantium.
ⓐ Archiepiskopou Kyprianou Plateia (next to the Archbishopric)
08.00–12.00, 14.00–16.00 Mon–Fri, 08.00–12.00 Sat (and during Mass)
Admission free

Archbishop's Palace

The resplendent palace of the Archbishop of Cyprus dates from 1960 and includes the modest private apartments of its first occupant, Archbishop Makarios, late Ethnarch of the Cypriot Orthodox Church and first President of the Republic of Cyprus. A gigantic statue of Makarios stands in the grounds.
ⓐ Archiepiskopou Kyprianou Plateia (within the Archbishopric)
Only open on Makarios's name day

Athalassa Forest Park

This park is a wide expanse of forest and fresh air on the city's doorstep. There are Forestry Service nurseries here, and a small lake with waterbirds and picnic areas. It makes a pleasant change of pace and scenery.
Off Leoforos Keryneias near the start of the motorway to Larnaka
Visitor centre: 22 46 29 43 10.00–15.00 Mon–Fri, 09.30–13.30 Sun (Sept–May); 08.00–14.30 Mon–Fri, closed weekends (June–Aug)
Admission charge to visitor centre

Byzantine Museum and Art Galleries

This museum displays an impressive Orthodox icon art and mosaic collection. Photography is forbidden, so leave your camera at the ticket office.
Archiepiskopou Kyprianou Plateia (within the Archbishopric)
22 43 06 67 09.00–16.30 Mon–Fri, 09.00–13.00 Sat, closed Sun
Admission charge

Cyprus Archaeological Museum

The museum takes you on a journey through time, by way of a superb collection of historical finds, beginning in the Stone Age around 7000 BC and ending at the downfall of the Roman Empire. The objects on display include 2,000 Bronze Age terracotta figurines found at the Sanctuary of Agia Eirini. Good spots for a shady picnic can be found among the trees of the Municipal Gardens.
Mouseiou Street 22 86 58 88 08.30–16.00 Tues–Sat, 08.30–17.00 Thur, 10.00–13.00 Sun Admission charge

Cyprus Classic Motorcycle Museum

Housing an impressive collection of 150 motorbikes dating from 1914 to 1983 including Archbishop Makarios's police escort bikes and motorcycles belonging to EOKA hero Stylianos Lenas and Turkish Cypriot champion Zeki Isa. There is also an exhibition of photographs.
44 Granikou Street 09.00–13.00, 15.00–19.00 Mon–Fri, 09.30–13.00 Sat Admission charge

Cyprus Folk Art Museum

Take a glimpse at the lifestyles of ordinary people in Cyprus during the 19th and early 20th centuries by visiting this collection of costumes, tapestry, embroidery, pottery and woodcarving.
ⓐ Archiepiskopou Kyprianou Plateia (within the Archbishopric)
ⓣ 22 43 25 78 ◔ 09.30–16.00 Tues–Fri, 09.00–13.00 Sat, closed Sun & Mon ❗ Admission charge

Eleftheria Monument (Liberty Monument)

This is a memorial to the struggle of the EOKA freedom fighters during the 1950s against British rule. It brought Cyprus to independence in 1960, although it did not bring the union with Greece for which EOKA had fought. Bronze statues representing priests and Cypriot civilians emerge from a marble prison as armed EOKA freedom fighters raise the bars.
ⓐ Podocataro Bastion of the Venetian Walls (off Leoforos Nikiforou Foka)

Famagusta Gate

One of three original fortified gateways in the Venetian walls, this one had fallen into disrepair before being restored and given a new lease of life as the city's Municipal Cultural Centre. You can visit temporary art exhibitions, experimental theatre and other cultural events in its stone-built galleries, and bar hop at trendy cafés in the area.
ⓐ Leoforos Athinas ⓣ 22 43 08 77 ◔ 10.00–13.00, 17.00–20.00 Mon–Fri (summer); 10.00–13.00, 16.00–19.00 Mon–Fri (winter), closed Sat & Sun ❗ Admission free

House of the Dragoman Hadjigeorgakis Kornesios

This splendid museum is housed in the restored 18th-century home of the Dragoman Hadjigeorgakis Kornesios, who met an untimely end in Istanbul in 1804. On the upper floor are rooms decorated in a style fit for a wealthy Ottoman official, including a divan-lined room. Downstairs are servants' quarters and storage rooms. Carved woodwork and colonnades add to the mansion's graceful lines.

ⓐ Patriarchou Grigoriou Street ⓣ 22 30 53 16 ⓛ 08.30–15.30 Mon–Fri, closed Sat & Sun ⓘ Admission charge

Human Rights Monument

Next to the Green Line at the end of Lidras Street is the poignant reminder of the Turkish invasion. The text of the UN Resolution on Human Rights is carved like a wheel at the base. Steel arrows pierce the text, representing the transgression of Cypriots' human rights.

ⓐ Northern end of Lidras Street ⓘ Information centre by monument

Ledra Palace

Once Lefkosia's most elegant hotel (and still sometimes called Ledra Palace Hotel), this is now a base of the United Nations peacekeeping force in Cyprus. You can see where it stands, though, inside the UN buffer zone, if you take the opportunity – not encouraged by the Greek Cypriot

House of the Dragoman Hadjigeorgakis Kornesios

THE GREEN LINE

Almost everyone wants to see this grim reminder of the divided state of Cyprus, which cuts like a wound through the heart of the old city of Lefkosia. The Green Line – so called because that was the colour of the pen used by United Nations peacekeepers to define the border on the map – runs through the city from east to west, a line of concrete-and-oil-drum barricades, ruined houses, sentry posts and fortified positions.

If you try to approach too close, you'll be stopped by the Cyprus National Guard before you get to the UN peacekeepers' positions in the middle of the two sides. Visitors can cross from the south to the north side of Lefkosia, and vice versa, at the **Ledra Palace Hotel** checkpoint.

authorities – to pass through Lefkosia's version of Berlin's former 'Checkpoint Charlie' and visit the Turkish zone of the city.
ⓐ Leoforos Markou Drakou (near Pafos Gate)

Ledra Street Observatory

Get a bird's-eye view of Lefkosia from the Shakolas Tower.
ⓣ 22 67 93 69 ◔ 10.00–20.00 (summer); 09.30–17.00 (winter)
❗ Admission charge

Leventis Municipal Museum

Situated within the renovated Laïki Geitonia district, the museum presents an interesting evocation of Lefkosia in times past.
ⓐ Ippokratous Street, Laïki Geitonia ⓣ 22 66 14 75 ◔ 10.00–16.30 Tues–Sun, closed Mon ❗ Admission free

Municipal Gardens

A cool place on a hot day, the park is shaded by trees and filled with flowers. You can sit on benches and stroll around on pathways, and visit fish

ponds and an aviary. Its open-air Garden Café is one of the oldest and most popular cafés in Lefkosia.
Ⓐ Off Leoforos Mouseiou (near Pafos Gate) and all around the city walls
Ⓛ Daily

National Struggle Museum

This museum is devoted to the Greek Cypriot movement for freedom from British colonial rule during the 1950s, led by the EOKA guerrilla organisation. Exhibits include weaponry, photographs, clandestine materials and a mock-up of an execution cell in which convicted EOKA killers were hanged by the authorities.
Ⓐ 7 Plateia Arch, Kyprianou Ⓣ 22 30 58 78 Ⓛ 08.00–14.00 Mon–Fri (also 15.00–17.30 Thur, except July & Aug) ⓘ Admission charge

Omeriye Hamam (Baths)

These baths were built in the 16th century by Lala Mustafa and given as a gift to the city. They have now been restored as part of the regeneration of the old city and offer visitors a range of relaxing treatments and massages.
Ⓐ Tillirias Plateia Ⓛ Women: 09.00–19.00 Wed, Fri, Sun; men: 09.00–19.00 Tues, Thur, Sat; closed Mon ⓘ Admission charge

Omeriye Mosque

A superb view of Lefkosia can be had from the minaret of this mosque, which, until the Ottoman conquest, had been a Catholic church. If you take off your shoes, you can visit the interior.
Ⓐ Trikoupi Plateia, Tillirias Ⓛ Daily ⓘ Admission free; donations

Pafos Gate

One of three historic gateways in the Venetian walls, Pafos Gate is overlooked by Turkish flags because the Green Line runs beside it. The gate is still an important traffic artery, connecting the old city with the new.
Ⓐ Pyli Pafou (at the north end of Leoforos Mouseiou)

Panagia Chrysaliniotissa Church

Our Lady of the Golden Flax is one of the oldest and most beautiful churches in Lefkosia, dating from the 15th century. Its dusky interior is embellished with icons and gilt ornamentation.

ⓐ Chrysaliniotissa Street ◷ Irregular hours

Plateia Eleftherias

Lefkosia's main square occupies a bridge over the dried-up moat around the Venetian walls and is a popular meeting place.

ⓐ Adjacent to Lidras Street, the main shopping thoroughfare in Lefkosia

Racecourse

Take a break from cultural tourism with an evening out at the horse races in the western suburb of Agios Dometios.

ⓐ Ippodromion Street ⓣ 22 78 27 27 ◷ Race meetings most Wed & Sat summer; Wed & Sun winter ❶ Admission charge

▲ *The Omeriye Hamam baths*

SHOPPING

The main shopping district in the old city is defined by Ledra Street and the parallel Onasagorou Street, as well as those streets that connect them. The trendiest is Stasikratous Street. Here you will find a good mix of upmarket and popular shops, with price tags to match. Outside the Venetian walls, the long Leoforos Archiepiskopou Makariou III has excellent shopping possibilities, with interesting boutiques in adjacent streets.

The best area of Lefkosia is found in Laïki Geitonia, an enclave of atmospheric tavernas with street terraces, attractively restored old buildings, and craft and souvenir shops, all in a pleasant, though busy, pedestrians-only zone. ⓐ Between Lidras Street and Aischylou Street, adjacent to Eleftheria Plateia

Cyprus Handicraft Centre The best of traditional handmade Cyprus products are on sale at this government-owned foundation. Its products are labelled 'CHS' and include pottery, woodcarving, handmade lace, loom embroidery and cotton work. There is also a workshop and exhibition centre, where traditional craftspeople can be seen in action. ⓐ 186 Leoforos Athalassis, in the southern suburbs, close to the Larnaka motorway access ⓣ 22 30 50 24

Markets An outdoor fruit and vegetable market is held every Wednesday morning at the Constanza Bastion of the Venetian walls. There are also permanent municipal markets at Dimarchias Square in the old city, and the junction of Leoforos Digeni Akrita with Leoforos Evgenias kai Antoniou Theodotou.

The Moufflon Probably the best English bookshop in Cyprus. They will search for, order and deliver books. A mine of local information. ⓐ 3 Sofouli Street ⓣ 22 66 51 55

State Collection of Contemporary Art

Modern paintings and sculptures by Cypriot artists.
ⓐ Leoforos Stasinou and Kritis Street ⓣ 22 30 49 47 ◷ 10.00–16.45 Mon–Fri, 10.00–12.45 Sat

Trypiotis Church

A richly embellished 17th-century church that was the favoured place of worship of Lefkosia's leading citizens in its time. Franco-Byzantine in style.
ⓐ Solonos Street ◷ Irregular hours

Venetian walls

Built by Cyprus's Venetian occupiers to defend against a long-awaited Ottoman invasion that finally came in 1570, the walls failed miserably to protect the city. The Turks stormed the walls and killed a reported 20,000 inhabitants. Still, the circular walls look strong enough even today and you can visit six of the eleven bastions that stand like gigantic pendants on the necklace of fortifications (the others are in the Turkish-occupied sector). Some sections of the moat have been laid out as gardens and make pleasant places for a stroll, especially during winter when they are filled with lush green grass and flowers.
ⓐ From the Pafos Gate to beyond the Famagusta Gate

TAKING A BREAK

Cafés £ ❶ You will find several trendy cafés in Lidras Street including the Greek chain Flo Café, Starbucks and Le Café, all serving a variety of coffees, ice creams, waffles and light meals. ⓐ Lidras Street

Restaurants

Aegeon ££ ❷ Although restaurants and cafés in the Famagusta Gate area are generally smart, stylish and pricey, Aegeon has managed to resist the temptation to follow suit and has remained true to its roots as a family taverna with fine traditional cooking. ⓐ 40 Ektoros Street ⓣ 22 43 32 97

Arhondiko ££ ❸ On a summer evening this is a romantic place where you can eat out of doors, enveloped in the glow of lanterns, gently serenaded by Greek music. ⓐ 27 Aristokyprou Street, Laïki Geitonia ⓣ 22 68 00 80

Erenias ££ ❹ Strovolos, once a village outside Lefkosia, has been swallowed up by the burgeoning capital. It's a bit out of town, but the trip is worth it, in particular for the *meze* served in surroundings of unpretentious charm. ⓐ 64a Leoforos Archiepiskopou Kyprianou, Strovolos ⓣ 22 42 28 60

Konatzin ££ ❺ Vegetarian restaurants are thin on the ground in Cyprus. Yet Konatzin serves a great vegetarian *meze* in the elegant setting of a converted town mansion with a garden terrace. ⓐ 10 Delfi Street ⓣ 22 77 69 90

Xefoto ££ ❻ A step up from the standard fare in the Laïki Geitonia district, Xefoto has an outside terrace and a stylish café-restaurant on the ground floor where a well-prepared, modern interpretation of Cypriot cuisine is served. ⓐ 6 Aischylou Street, Laïki Geitonia ⓣ 22 66 65 67

AFTER DARK

There are a number of good cinemas showing international films (mostly American) in their original language with Greek subtitles. Among them is the **Zena Palace**, at Theofanos Theodotou Street near Plateia Eleftherias, with **Pantheon** and **Opera** cinemas close by.

Brew Lounge & Tea Bar ❼ is a trendy cocktail bar frequented by artists and writers at night and a tea house serving 25 exotic teas and snacks by day. ⓐ 30b Hippocrates Street ⓣ 22 10 01 33

Zoo Club ❽ is a lively café and club. ⓐ 15 Stasinou Avenue ⓣ 22 45 88 11

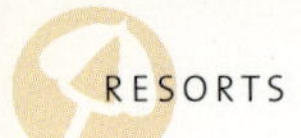

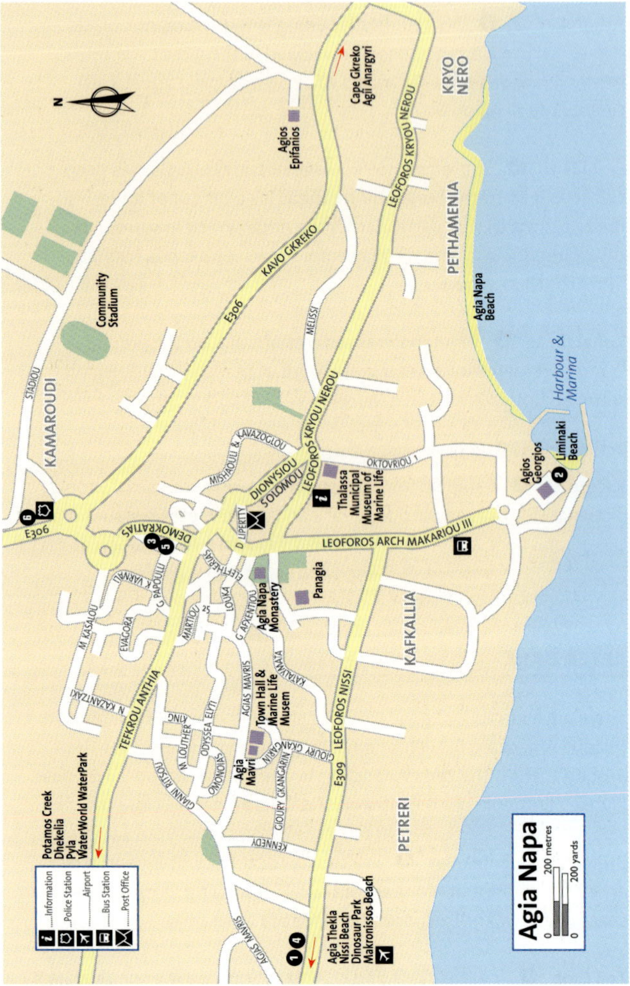
Agia Napa
0 200 metres
0 200 yards
Information
Police Station
Airport
Bus Station
Post Office
Potamos Creek
Dhekelia
Pyla
WaterWorld WaterPark
Agia Thekla
Nissi Beach
Dinosaur Park
Makronissos Beach
Cape Gkreko
Agii Anargyri
Community Stadium
KAMAROUDI
PETRERI
KAFKALLIA
PETHAMENIA
KRYO NERO
Agios Epifanios
Agia Napa Beach
Harbour & Marina
Liminaki Beach
Agios Georgios
Thalassa Municipal Museum of Marine Life
Panagia
Agia Napa Monastery
Town Hall & Marine Life Musem
Agia Mavri
E306
E309
KAVO GKREKO
LEOFOROS KRYOU NEROU
LEOFOROS ARCH MAKARIOU III
LEOFOROS NISSI
TEFKROU ANTHIA
STADIOU
MELISSI
OKTOVRIOU 1
DIONYSIOU SOLOMOU
MISHAOULI & KAVAZOGLOU
DEMOKRATIAS
D LIPERTIS
ELEFTHERIAS
LOUKA
C AFXENTIOU
MARTIOU 25
G. PAPOULLI
K VARNALI
EVAGORA
M. KASALOU
N KAZANTZAKI
AGIAS MAVRIS
KATALYMATA
M. LOUTHER KING
ODYSSEA ELYTI
OMONOIAS
GIANNI RITSOU
GIOURY GKANGARIN
KENNEDY

Agia Napa (Ayia Napa)

Set in the red earth of the Kokkinochoria district northeast of Larnaka, Agia Napa was once a sleepy fishing harbour dating back to 1366, but is now a modern beach resort built for fun in the sun. Its focal points are the bustling Seferi Plateia, the harbour and, of course, the beaches, some of which lie just outside the resort itself. Agia Napa's tourist information office is at Leoforos Kryou Nerou. ⓣ 23 72 17 96

BEACHES

Agia Napa Beach

Very convenient beach on the bay east of the harbour. In two sections, Pethamenia and Kryo Nero, ending at the Thalassines Spilies (Sea Caves).

Makronissos Beach

The last in the chain of beaches west of Agia Napa, with an excavated warren of ancient Greek and Roman tombs, free and open to the public.

Nissi Beach

The best of a cluster of good – but very busy – beaches lying a few kilometres west of Agia Napa. Easily reachable by bus from the resort, there are good watersports and other beach facilities here.

THINGS TO SEE & DO

Agia Napa harbour and marina

The fishing boats, tour boats, glass-bottomed boats and private yachts make for a busy and colourful scene. In front of the harbour, the tiny, whitewashed chapel of Agios Georgios looks out of place amid the tourist clutter.

ⓐ End of Leoforos Archiepiskopou Makariou III

Agia Napa Monastery

A cool and tranquil place to escape the crowds, with a pretty fountain, some shade-giving trees, including a 600-year-old sycamore, and a handful of ageing nuns in attendance.

ⓐ Beside Seferi Plateia ◷ Dawn–dusk ❗ Admission free

Agia Thekla

A whitewashed chapel overlooking the sea near Nissi Bay. An older chapel, dug into the rocks nearby, has a few icons illuminated only by an oil lamp.

◷ Open permanently

Agii Anargyri

A small chapel beside the sea north of Cape Greko, at the end of a rough track off the main road. Its dazzling white makes a nice contrast with the sea's deep blue. The sandy beach along a shallow bay a little further north is one of the best on this stretch of coast.

Cape Gkreko

This cape is at the tip of a long peninsula southeast of Agia Napa, lined by dramatic cliffside scenery. An overlook that you can reach on foot from a parking area near the cape gives a dramatic view along the rugged coastline towards Agia Napa. The cape and the lighthouse at its tip are fenced off because of nearby military and civilian communications facilities. Experienced snorkellers and divers explore the waters around here – but it is an unsuitable place for inexperienced amateurs.

Dhekelia

One of the two British Sovereign Bases in Cyprus is located here (the other is at Episkopi/Akrotiri, west of Lemesos). It is a very British residential area, with street names such as Waterloo Road.

Dinosaur Park

Models of prehistoric creatures that lived millions of years ago, complete with sounds, are on display at this family attraction.

ⓐ Off Leoforos Nissi ⓣ 22 84 32 23 ◷ 11.00–13.00, 16.00–24.00 (June–Nov)

Potamos Creek

Small fishing boats crowd into this creek harbour near Liopetri village, creating a colourful and tranquil scene. The fishermen themselves eat in the two harbourside tavernas, where fish is fresh off the boats. You can cycle to the harbour along the coastal road that runs west from Makronissos beach.

Pyla

Greek and Turkish Cypriots still live in harmony in this village on the edge of Britain's Dhekelia Sovereign Base Area. There is an Orthodox church and a mosque, a Turkish coffee shop and a Greek *kafenion*, all watched over by UN peacekeepers. A 16th-century Venetian watchtower stands on the rugged Cape Pyla coast.

Thalassa Municipal Museum of Marine Life

Themed on the marine life around Cyprus's coast, this museum also includes a replica of a 4th-century BC Greek vessel.

RED EARTH

The countryside around Agia Napa is called the Kokkinochoria (Red Villages) district. Its irrigated red soil produces three crops a year of the Cyprus potatoes that are so popular in Britain. Not so long ago, windmills that used to draw water from underground sources were abandoned in favour of diesel pumps. Now, some of those once rusting windmills are being restored and brought back into use again, creating a handsome sight.

ⓐ Agia Napa Town Hall, 25 Agias Mavris Street ⓣ 23 72 34 09
ⓛ 09.00–14.00 Mon–Fri, 09.00–13.00 Sat ⓘ Admission charge

WaterWorld WaterPark

Kamikaze slides, river tube rides and rolling logs guarantee the children will be amused at this well-equipped aqua park. Adults can relax at the beach, or at the poolside bars and restaurants.
ⓐ 18 Agia Thekla Road ⓣ 23 72 44 44 ⓦ www.waterworldwaterpark.com
ⓛ 10.00–18.00 May–Sept, 10.00–17.00 Apr & Oct ⓘ Admission charge

EXCURSION

Take a boat trip from the harbour along the coast to see the sad but fascinating sight of Varosha, a suburb of Famagusta that was once Cyprus's main tourist resort. Under Turkish occupation since 1974, it has been totally deserted and is literally crumbling to the ground.

TAKING A BREAK

Ji-Li ££ ❶ Serves authentic Chinese and Cantonese food in pretty, traditional surroundings. Has over 100 specialities on the menu, plus takeaway service. Friendly staff. ⓐ 48 Leoforos Nissi, on the junction of Agias Mavris Street ⓣ 23 72 20 22

Markos Taverna ££ ❷ A harbourside taverna specialising in fresh local fish and fish *meze*. Also serves local homemade Cypriot specialities and vegetarian dishes. ⓐ Agia Napa Harbour ⓣ 23 72 58 77

Stamna Tavern ££ ❸ A charming taverna serving traditional local dishes, cooked and served by the family in Agia Napa's oldest house. ⓐ Demokratias Street ⓣ 23 72 13 86

Taverna Mangas ££ ❹ Family-orientated restaurant serving international food and typical Cypriot dishes. ⓐ Leoforos Nissi (opposite Sunwing Hotel) ⓣ 23 72 29 76

Nissi beach, near Agia Napa

Taverna Napa ££ ❺ A rustic taverna with outside terrace, established since 1976, serving excellent local dishes such as *souvlaki* and *kleftiko* – add your signature to the hundreds decorating the walls. ⓐ 15 Demokratias Street ⓣ 23 72 12 80

To Ploumin ££ ❻ One of the area's best tavernas, in a 1930s village house decorated with traditional household and farming implements, and with a listed windmill. Home cooking uses fresh ingredients from surrounding farms. ⓐ 28 Oktovriou Street ⓣ 23 73 04 44

AFTER DARK

A mecca for partygoers, Agia Napa boasts enough nightlife to make your head spin! Party in the central square at night, later following the crowds to popular haunts **Carwash**, **Moods** and **River Reggae**.

Protaras

Along with the related resort of Pernera, Protaras occupies the furthest southeastern corner of Cyprus accessible to visitors. A little further up the road is the UN buffer zone. It is a purpose-built family resort area, quieter than Agia Napa, with a beach reputed to be one of the best on the island. Along this ruggedly beautiful stretch of coastline there used to be nothing except a few fishing harbours and some little country churches.

BEACHES

Konnos Beach

Lying southeast of Protaras, at the edge of the scenic Cape Greko area, the facilities include sunbeds, beach umbrellas, pedalos and paragliding. Accessible by bus from Protaras.

Pernera Beach

Pernera is a northward extension of Protaras, separated from it by a zone of citrus orchards and connected by road.

Protaras Beach and Fig Tree Bay

These two stretches of beach run into each other along the front of Protaras, and are reached by several side roads.

THINGS TO SEE & DO

You'll see just about everything there is to do in Protaras as soon as you look out of your hotel room window in the morning at the sun rising out of the sea. The thing to do here is to head for the beach. In addition, there are some easy bicycle or walking trips to make, in and around the resort, including to Paralimni and Agias Trias harbours to see the fishing boats, and to Profitis Ilias church, not so much for the little church itself as for the view from the hill on which it stands.

Profitis Ilias has wonderful views of the coast

Ammochostos (Famagusta) viewpoints

There are several places around Dherynia from where you can view the abandoned city of Famagusta. **Annita's View Point** is a popular location, and provides binoculars and information. Famagusta Beach View and the Cultural Centre of Occupied Famagusta are two more. You can take a visual 'tour' of Varosha, a crumbling and deserted suburb of Famagusta that was once Cyprus's main tourist resort. Varosha can also be visited by boat (see page 30).

Watersports

Being the main attraction of the resorts, the beaches in the area of Protaras, Pernera, Fig Tree Bay and Konnos Bay have a full range of watersports facilities.

EXCURSIONS

Agia Trias

North of Pernera, a side road to the right off the main coast road leads to a pleasant sandy bay and a cluster of seaside tavernas beside a small chapel.

SHOPPING

GT For good-quality Italian leather goods at factory prices, on Hotel Road, near the Sunrise Hotel. ⓣ 23 83 12 24

La Lenia For ladies' fashion accessories, jewellery, leather goods, watches, perfumes, etc. The company has four different boutiques in Protaras, all on Hotel Road. ⓣ 23 83 22 70

Dheryneia

This inland village is jammed up against the demarcation line. From the Viewpoint Café's observation tower you can look with binoculars and a telescope across the UN buffer zone to the Turkish-occupied part of Cyprus, in the direction of Varosha. A **Folk Art Museum** contains farming tools and household items from past centuries.

ⓐ 2 Demetris Lipertis Street ◷ 09.00–13.00, 16.00–18.00 Mon–Sat

ⓘ Admission charge

Paralimni

Having grown substantially in recent years, this town still offers some traditional Cypriot character in an area that is otherwise notable only for its tourist resorts. The main square consists of a cluster of impressive churches surrounded by cafés and tavernas. West of the town is Paralimni Lake, which fills up with water during winter and dries out to a muddy swamp in summer.

Profitis Ilias

Midway between Protaras and Pernera, on the left side of the road, this small and handsome church commands a fine view of the coast.

TAKING A BREAK

Anatolia ££ Despite its Turkish-sounding name, this is a Greek Cypriot taverna, serving excellent food, which specialises in that most Cypriot of meals, the many small dishes of a *meze* – a great way to sample the traditional fare. It also offers international dishes. ⓐ Agios Elias ⓣ 23 83 15 33

China House Restaurant ££ This is one of the biggest original Chinese restaurants in Cyprus. Diners can choose from more than a hundred different dishes served in ornate surroundings. ⓐ Xenodohion Avenue ⓣ 23 83 22 57

Nicolas Tavern ££ A traditional Cypriot taverna serving specialities cooked in an authentic wood clay oven, fish, vegetarian *meze* and wines from regional wineries. ⓐ Xenodohion Avenue ⓣ 23 83 30 84

Sao Paulo ££ For something truly unique, try this family restaurant serving great Brazilian and Italian cuisine – the only one of its kind in Cyprus! Sea view and special children's menus. ⓐ Hotel Road ⓣ 23 83 26 10

Spartiatis ££ This restaurant specialises in seafood fresh from the nearby harbour and traditional Greek dishes, serving it all up in a quiet, romantic atmosphere. ⓐ Konnos Beach ⓣ 23 83 13 86

AFTER DARK

Protaras boasts a number of bars, pubs and clubs, including the longest-running and most popular nightclub in the area, **Boogies Disco**. Its **Sfinx Bar** is legendary. Other favourites for partying include the clubs **Return of the Kings**, **Knights** and **Niata**.

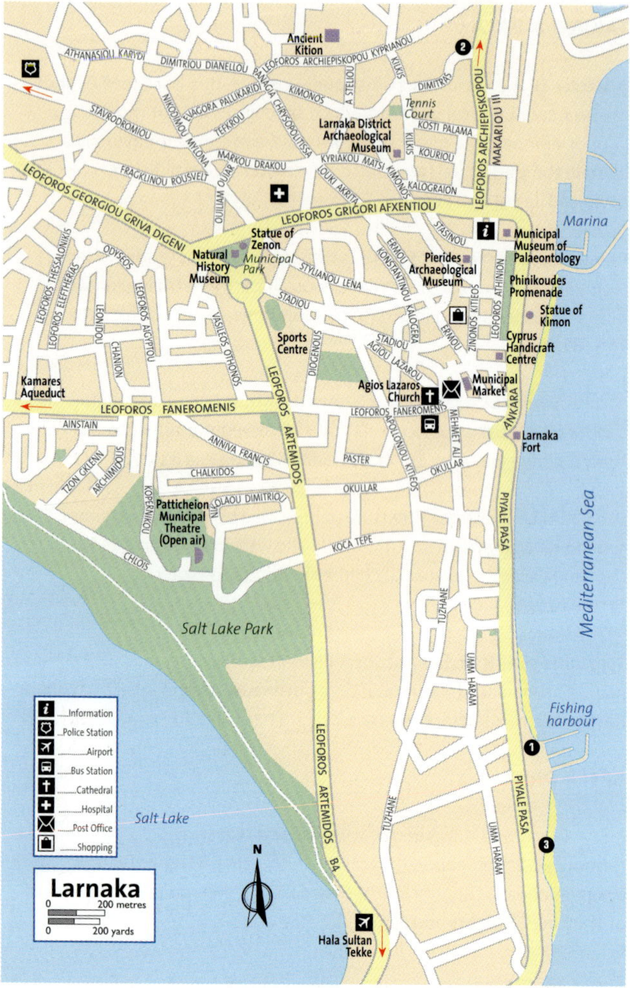

Larnaka

0 200 metres
0 200 yards

Symbol	Meaning
i	Information
	Police Station
	Airport
	Bus Station
	Cathedral
	Hospital
	Post Office
	Shopping

Ancient Kition
Tennis Court
Larnaka District Archaeological Museum
Marina
Municipal Museum of Palaeontology
Statue of Zenon
Natural History Museum
Municipal Park
Pierides Archaeological Museum
Phinikoudes Promenade
Statue of Kimon
Sports Centre
Cyprus Handicraft Centre
Kamares Aqueduct
Agios Lazaros Church
Municipal Market
Larnaka Fort
Patticheion Municipal Theatre (Open air)
Mediterranean Sea
Salt Lake Park
Fishing harbour
Salt Lake
Hala Sultan Tekke
N

ATHANASIOU KARYDI
DIMITRIOU DIANELLOU
LEOFOROS ARCHIEPISKOPOU KYPRIANOU
PANAGIA
KIMONOS
A STELIOU
KILKIS
DIMITRAS
STAVRODROMIOU
EVAGORA PALLIKARIDI
NIKODIMOU MYLONA
TEFKROU
CHRYSOPOLITISSA
KOSTI PALAMA
KOURIOU
LEOFOROS ARCHIEPISKOPOU MAKARIOU III
MARKOU DRAKOU
KYRIAKOU MATSI
FRAGKLINOU ROUSVELT
OUILIAM OUIAR
LOUKI AKRITA
KIMONOS
KALOGRAION
LEOFOROS GEORGIOU GRIVA DIGENI
LEOFOROS GRIGORI AFXENTIOU
STASINOU
ODYSSEOS
ERMOU
KONSTANTINOU KALOGERA
STYLIANOU LENA
LEOFOROS THESSALONIKIS
LEOFOROS ELEFTHERIAS
LEOFOROS AIGYPTOU
LEONIDOU
CHANION
VASILEOS OTHONOS
STADIOU
DIOGENOUS
ZINONOS KITIEOS
LEOFOROS ATHINION
AGIOU LAZAROU
LEOFOROS FANEROMENIS
LEOFOROS ARTEMIDOS
ANKARA
AINSTAIN
ANNIVA FRANCIS
MEHMET ALI
APOLLONIOU KITIEOS
PASTER
OKULLAR
CHALKIDOS
TZON GKLENN
ARCHIMIDOUS
KOPERNIKOU
NIKOLAOU DIMITRIOU
PIYALE PASA
KOCA TEPE
CHLOIS
TUZHANE
UMM HARAM
LEOFOROS ARTEMIDOS B4
1
2
3

Larnaka (Larnaca)

The third-biggest town in Cyprus, with a population of some 60,000, Larnaka is a busy commercial centre as well as being a holiday resort. There are plenty of visitor attractions in the centre and a reasonable beach adjoining the seafront promenade. Other beach and watersports facilities lie outside town to the south and the east, along Larnaka Bay. Larnaka has two tourist information offices:

Airport tourist office ⓐ International Airport ⓣ 24 64 35 76

Cyprus Tourist Organisation office ⓐ Vasileos Pavlou Plateia ⓣ 24 65 43 22.

BEACHES

While there is a reasonable beach on the Larnaka seafront, most of the coastal action in town takes place along curving Larnaka Bay on the Larnaka–Dhekelia road. In addition to a long stretch of Blue Flag beaches, lined with a full range of watersports possibilities, there are cafés, tavernas and shops.

THINGS TO SEE & DO

Agios Lazaros church

The 9th-century Orthodox church has a beautiful 17th-century gilded iconostasis (altar screen) and the sepulchre of St Lazarus, who was raised from the dead by Jesus. There is also a small Byzantine museum in the church grounds, showing icons and other religious items.

ⓐ Agiou Lazarou Street ⓣ 24 65 24 98 ⓛ 08.30–12.30, 15.30–18.30 (Apr–Aug); 08.00–12.30, 14.30–17.00 (Sept–Mar)

Ancient Kition

Birthplace of the philosopher Zenon, ancient Kition has almost entirely vanished, thanks to the British, who carted away most of the ruins during the 19th century for use as building materials in Egypt. In this

once important Greek, Phoenician and Roman city, you can just about identify the straggly remains of a Phoenician temple to the goddess Astarte, which burned down in 312 BC. A *stele* (grave marker) found on the site carries an inscription boasting of the power of the Assyrian King Sargon II, who conquered Cyprus in 709 BC.
ⓐ Off Leontiou Machaira Street ⓛ 09.00–14.30 Mon–Fri, also 15.00–17.00 Thur (except July & Aug) ⓘ Admission charge

Fishing harbour

See fishermen land their catch every morning at this colourful harbour.
ⓐ Piyale Pasha near Larnaka Fort

Hala Sultan Tekke

This mosque nestles in a grove of palm trees by the shore of Larnaka's Salt Lake. Although it dates from the early 18th century, it incorporates the tomb of Hala Sultan, also known as Umm Haram, a relative of the Prophet Mohammed who died in Cyprus in AD 649. The sepulchre is covered in green cloths of mourning (see page 72).
ⓛ 07.30–19.30 (summer); 09.00–17.00 (winter); 09.00–18.00 (spring and autumn) ⓘ Admission free; donations welcome

Kamares Aqueduct

Altogether 33 arches survive from this aqueduct, southwest of Larnaka, built by the Ottomans in the 18th century to bring water to Larnaka from the Troodos foothills.
ⓐ Beside the Larnaka–Lemesos Road on the edge of the city

Larnaka District Archaeological Museum

This museum houses a selection of pottery, coins, bronzes and statuary, with a noteworthy collection from nearby historic sites such as Kition and Choirokoitia.
ⓐ Kalograion Plateia, near Larnaka Tennis Club ⓣ 24 30 41 69
ⓛ 09.00–14.30 Mon–Fri, also Thur 15.00–17.00 (except during summer)
ⓘ Admission charge

Larnaka Harbour

Larnaka Fort

The 17th-century Larnaka Fort occupies a dramatic position overlooking the sea and houses a medieval museum, displaying suits of armour and other historical objects.

Ⓐ Phinikoudes Promenade Ⓣ 24 30 45 76 Ⓛ 09.00–19.30 (summer); 09.00–17.00 (winter); 09.00–18.00 (spring and autumn); closed Sat & Sun ❶ Admission charge

Marina

In Larnaka Marina, cabin cruisers, yachts, glass-bottomed cruise boats and excursion cruisers are lined up side by side.

Ⓐ Beside Vasileos Pavlou Plateia

Municipal Museum of Palaeontology

Just the thing for children who can't get enough of dinosaurs. Housed in five former customs stores that date back to the period of British rule in the early 19th century.

Ⓐ Municipal Cultural Centre, Europa Plateia

Ⓣ 24 62 85 87 Ⓛ 09.00–14.00 Tues–Fri, 09.00–12.00 Sat & Sun (closed Sun June–Aug)

Municipal Park

Larnaka, like other Cypriot towns, is short of green spaces, which makes this small triangle of trees, plants and grass in the town centre a doubly welcome source of shade on a hot, dusty day. The Municipal Library and Natural History Museum stand in the grounds.

ⓐ Leoforos Grigori Afxentiou ⓛ Open permanently

Natural History Museum

Collections from the natural world in Cyprus, such as local reptiles, birds, insects, fossils and marine life species.

ⓐ Leoforos Grigori Afxentiou (situated inside Larnaka Municipal Park) ⓣ 24 65 25 69 ⓛ 10.00–13.00, 16.00–18.00 Tues–Sun (June–Aug); 10.00–13.00, 15.00–17.00 (Sept–May), closed Mon ⓘ Admission charge

Phinikoudes Promenade

A handsome stretch of walkway along the seafront from the Marina almost as far as Larnaka Fort, lined with palm trees, smart, open-air cafés and restaurants. A bust of the ancient Athenian hero Kimon, who lost his life in an unsuccessful attempt to free the city from the Persians, stands on the promenade.

Pierides Archaeological Museum

A private archaeological museum operated by the Pierides Foundation, housed in a 19th-century mansion. It displays pottery, ornaments and statues from the Stone Age to the end of the Roman Empire.

ⓐ 4 Zinonos Kitieos Street ⓣ 24 81 45 55 ⓛ 09.00–16.00 Mon–Thur, 09.00–13.00 Fri & Sat, closed Sun ⓘ Admission charge

Statues of Kimon and Zenon

The bust of General Kimon, who died attempting to liberate Cyprus from Persian rule in 450 BC, can be seen on the palm-lined promenade. The philosopher Zenon, who was born in ancient Kition, now Larnaka, in the 4th century BC, is also honoured at the Municipal Park.

ⓐ Phinikoudes Promenade

SHOPPING

Cyprus Handicraft Centre The only Larnaka branch of the government-operated handicrafts foundation. ⓐ 6 Kosma Lysioti Street ⓣ 24 30 43 27

Fruit market Located in the middle of the old Turkish quarter, this small but busy fruit and vegetable market is worth a visit. ⓐ Ermou Street

Laïki Geitonia (Geitonia) Arts and crafts and good souvenir shops. ⓐ One street behind the seafront, near the Larnaka Fort

Tofarides Bookshop Books in English and other languages, along with cards and more. ⓐ 45–47 Zinonos Kitieos Street ⓣ 24 65 49 12

Walking tours

Every Wednesday at 10.00, there is a free walking tour of Larnaka: 'Larnaka Past and Present', starting at the Cyprus Tourist Organisation office at Vasileos Pavlou Plateia on the seafront. Every Friday at 10.00, there is a free tour of the craft district of Scala, beginning at Larnaka Fort. ⓣ 24 65 43 22

TAKING A BREAK

Zephyros ££ ❶ Overlooking the colourful fishing harbour, this taverna serves one of the best fish *mezes* in town. ⓐ 37 Piyale Pasa ⓣ 24 62 43 17

Masalas ££–£££ ❷ An excellent Indian restaurant with an outdoor terrace and darkly atmospheric interior. Though the menu is relatively short, the dishes are carefully prepared, with prompt and friendly service. ⓐ Larnaka–Dhekelia road ⓣ 24 64 49 50

Varashiotis £££ ❸ Popular with Larnaka's élite, this restaurant serves up great sea views and freshly caught fish and seafood. Fish soup is a speciality. ⓐ 7 Piyale Pasa ⓣ 77 77 77 08

Lemesos
0 250 metres
0 250 yards
Information
Police Station
Airport
Bus Station
Post Office
Shopping
N
Mediterranean Sea
Wooden Pier
Wooden Pier
Old Harbour
Municipal Gardens
Archaeological Museum
Municipal Folk Art Museum
Cyprus Handicraft Service
Sea Front Promenade (Sculpture Park)
Market
Lemesos Castle & Cyprus Medieval Museum
Carob Museum
TURKISH QUARTER
Wine Museum
Fasouri Watermania
LEOFOROS ARCHIEPISKOPOU MAKARIOU III
OKTOVRIOU 28
CHRISTODOULOU CHATZIPAVLOU
SPYROU ARAOUZOU
SYNTAGMATOS
GLADSTONOS
AGIAS ZONIS
AGIAS FYLAXEOS
EIRINIS
ANEXARTISIAS
PANAGIOTI SYMEOU
LORDOU VYRONOS
TZON KENNENTY
AGIOU ANDREOU
ELEFTHERIOU VENIZELOU
IEROUSALIM
ANDROUTSOU
KARAISKAKI
EVRIPIDOU
EVANGELISTRIAS
THEKLAS A LYSIOTI
KOSTA PARTASSIDI
ARCHIMIDOUS
ANAXAGORA
STASINOU
KAPODISTRIA
ZINONOS
PAVLOU MELA
VASILEIOU MAKEDONOS
THEMIDOS
ATHINON
KITIOU KYPRIANOU
ELLADOS
AGKYRAS
VRAGADINOU
NAVARINOU
IPPARCHOU
VASILI MICHAILIDI
IRAKLEOUS
THESSALONIKIS
LEONTIOU MACHAIRA
VICTOROS OUGKO
ELEFTHERIAS
KLEOPATRAS
ZALONGOU
BAGIAZIT
FERZI PASA
1 10 12 2 7 8 9 4 3 5 6 11 13

Lemesos (Limassol)

Cyprus's second-largest city, after Lefkosia, Lemesos (also known as Limassol) combines an industrial and shipping role with that of a seaside resort. There are plenty of things to see and do, and an active dining, nightlife and cultural scene, with a 15-km (9-mile) coastline stretching between Amathus and the old town. Lemesos has three tourist information offices: **Downtown office** ⓐ 115A Spyrou Araouzou Street ⓣ 25 36 27 56; **Germasogeia office** ⓐ 22 Georgiou A' Street ⓣ 25 32 32 11; **Lemesos harbour office** ⓣ 25 57 18 68.

BEACHES

Lemesos Beach and promenade runs more or less the full length of Lemesos's seafront adjoining Oktovriou 28 Street. It has loungers, beach umbrellas and pedalos.

THINGS TO SEE & DO

Archaeological Museum

This museum houses many important finds from the ancient Greek and Roman cities of Amathous and Kourion. Among the treasures are statues of Aphrodite and of Egyptian and Phoenician gods.
ⓐ 5 Anastasi Sioukri and Vyronos Street ⓣ 25 30 51 57 ⓛ 09.00–19.00 Tues, Wed, Fri, 08.00–15.00 Thur, 08.00–17.00 Sat, closed Sun ⓘ Admission charge

Boat tours

Take cruises from Lemesos Old Harbour, around Akrotiri Peninsula. Several tour companies also operate glass-bottomed boats.

Carob Museum

This restored carob mill, built in 1900, houses the machinery used to process one of Cyprus's main exports at that time, and an exhibitions area.
ⓐ Next to the castle ⓣ 25 76 28 28 ⓛ Daily until late

FASOURI WATERMANIA

A great day out for the family, on 17 hectares (42 acres), this attraction has a huge wave pool, water slides that include a kamikaze slide, a Lazy River, adult and children's pools, restaurant, cafeteria and snack bars. ⓐ Trahoni Village Road ⓣ 25 71 42 35 ⓦ www.fasouri-watermania.com ◷ 10.00–18.00 May–Sept, 10.00–17.00 Oct ❗ Admission charge. Shuttle buses operate from main resorts to the park

Lemesos Castle & Cyprus Medieval Museum

The castle is a battlemented affair that was originally built during the Crusader era in the 12th century by the Lusignan kings. Venetians, Turks and the British all added bits and pieces to it and changed others. Nowadays the arched stone halls in its interior house the Cyprus Medieval Museum, displaying weapons, sculptures and other items from that period.

ⓐ Off Eirinis Street near the Old Harbour ⓣ 25 30 54 19 ◷ 09.00–17.00 Mon–Sat, 10.00–13.00 Sun ❗ Admission charge

Municipal Folk Art Museum

Mementoes of a mostly vanished Cypriot lifestyle, in a 19th-century mansion, including all kinds of work and household objects and furnishings that were in use until recent times.

ⓐ 253 Agiou Andreou Street ⓣ 25 36 23 03 ◷ 08.30–13.30, 16.00–18.30 Mon–Fri (June–Sept); 15.00–17.30 Mon–Fri (Oct–May), closed Thur afternoon ❗ Admission charge

Old Harbour

This is Lemesos's small-scale fishing and yacht harbour, from which the coastal tour boats leave. It is located near the castle, at the end of the seafront promenade.

Turkish quarter

When you come out of Lemesos Castle you are in the old Turkish quarter of the city. It is well worth strolling around its narrow streets for an hour. Among the monuments in this area are the Djami Kebir Mosque, the Köprülü Haji Ibrahim Mosque and a Turkish bath-house. Some of the elegant Ottoman-style houses have Turkish inscriptions.

Wine Museum

Learn about the history of wine production in Cyprus and view medieval vessels and old documents.

ⓐ Pafos Road near Erimi village ⓣ 25 87 38 08 ⓛ 09.00–17.00 Mon–Sat
ⓘ Admission charge

TAKING A BREAK

Hamlet £ ❶ An English-style pub with a friendly, relaxed, family atmosphere. Bar snacks are also served. ⓐ 72b Leoforos Amathous ⓣ 25 32 08 52

Ship Inn £ ❷ If you need your full British breakfast and familiar dishes for lunch and dinner, this is a good place to go. The sea view adds atmosphere to what is already a family-orientated and friendly place. ⓐ Kerkyra Street ⓣ 25 58 21 80

Aliada ££ ❸ A cosy restaurant in a beautifully restored house, this place has an extensive menu of local produce, home-made soups, a great cold buffet, and charcoaled meat and fish. ⓐ 117 Eirinis Street ⓣ 25 34 07 58

Meze Taverna ££ ❹ This popular taverna offers a great *meze* of 25 different dishes and excellent service. Also dishes for vegetarians. ⓐ 209 Agiou Andreou Street ⓣ 25 36 73 33

SHOPPING

Bustling and cosmopolitan Lemesos has plenty of shopping, dining-out and nightlife opportunities. Most of these are situated conveniently within the relatively small city centre and along the seafront, although others are in the nearby resort suburb of Germasogeias.

Cyprus Handicraft Service The only Lemesos branch of the government-operated handicrafts foundation. ⓐ 25 Themidos Street ⓣ 25 30 51 18

Markets There are two fruit and vegetable markets, both of them located near the Cyprus Tourism Organisation office. ⓐ Genethliou Mitella Street and Saripolou Street

Marks & Spencer Do not expect the full range of goods found in the big British stores of this UK-based firm – but you will find good-quality clothes. ⓐ Leoforos Nykiforou Grigora ⓣ 25 74 81 66

Theodoros Theodorou Design Jewellery Exquisitely designed jewellery with prices to match. ⓐ 34c Anexartisias Street ⓣ 25 36 99 33

Debenhams A well-known department store chain throughout Cyprus (and the UK) that offers an upmarket selection of goods, its prices remain keen and the store is popular with locals and tourists alike. Best buys include clothes, cosmetics, food and ceramics souvenirs. Lemesos has two branches: ⓐ Apollon, Petrou Tsirou Street ⓣ 25 83 18 31; ⓐ Olympia, Oktovriou 28 Street ⓣ 25 59 11 33

Lemesos harbour

Neo Phaliro ££ ❺ Highly regarded by local diners for its excellent local and international food and uncompromising Cypriot character. ⓐ 135 Gladstonos Street ⓣ 25 36 57 68

Porta ££ ❻ How do you feel about eating in a renovated donkey stable? Designer class and good taste characterise this restaurant in the old Turkish quarter. ⓐ 17 Genethliou Mitella Street ⓣ 25 36 03 39

Scotties Steakhouse ££ ❼ This restaurant specialises in steaks – good ones – making this a popular place. ⓐ 38 Souliou Street ⓣ 25 57 51 73

Ta Piatakia ££ ❽ Sample Cypriot cuisine with a twist at this cosy restaurant. There are up to 30 delightful dishes on the menu and you

Lemesos – a bustling shipping city

get personal service from the owner. Duck with walnuts is a signature dish. ⓐ 7 Nicodemou Mylona ⓣ 25 74 50 17

Trata ££ ❾ A family-run restaurant that serves excellent *mezes* of fish straight from the boats, all at a good price. ⓐ 4 Ioanni Tompazi Street, Debenhams Olympia complex ⓣ 25 58 66 00

Blue Island £££–£££ ⓾ For a special evening out, this is one of the classiest restaurants in the Lemesos area, serving French and international cuisine in a somewhat formal setting. There is a shaded, vine-covered patio/garden for outdoor dining. ⓐ 3 Leoforos Amathountos, old Lemesos–Lefkosia road ⓣ 25 32 14 66

Carob Mill Restaurants ££–£££ ⓫ This restored complex features some of the liveliest and trendiest bars and restaurants in town. Make up your own *meze* at Karatello, enjoy Mediterranean dishes at fashionable Stretto, relax at chic Artima and spend time lingering over a beer distilled at the Draught Microbrewery. ⓐ Lanitis Carob Mill, Vasilissis, Old Harbour (behind castle) ⓣ 25 82 04 30

Xydas £££ ⓬ First-class seafood restaurant that serves fresh (as opposed to frozen) fish. ⓐ 22 Anthemidos Street, Amathous ⓣ 25 72 83 36

AFTER DARK

Lemesos's extended seafront is the place to go for pubs, clubs and bars. Whether you're in the mood for robust partying or for a quiet drink with the family, you'll find the perfect place somewhere along this lively stretch. Many bars also show live international sporting events.

Fabrique ⓭ This bar in the Old Town has traditional live music. ⓐ Agkyras Street, near the castle ⓛ 09.00–dawn

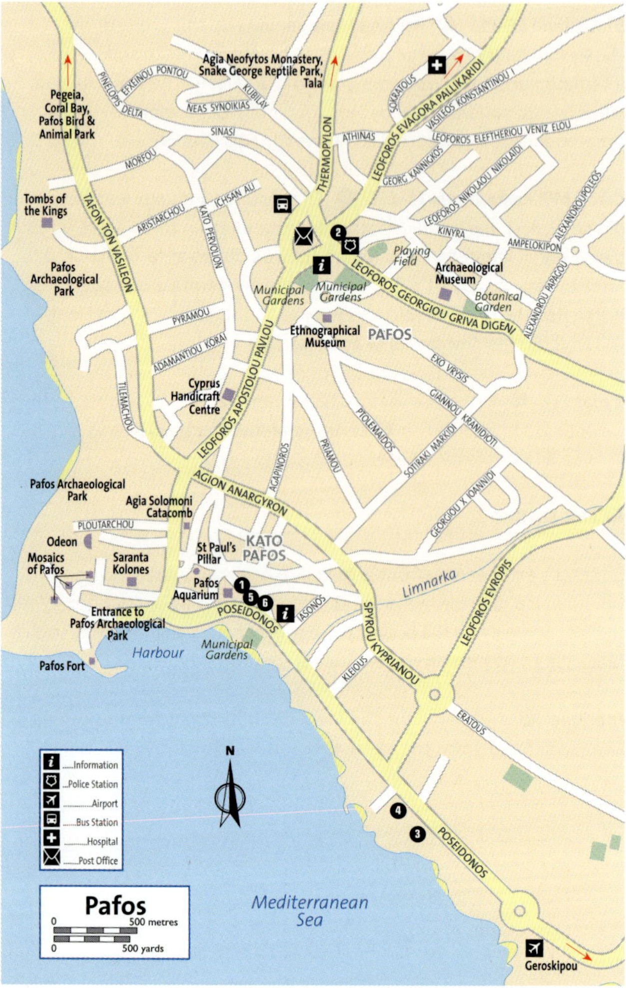

Agia Neofytos Monastery, Snake George Reptile Park, Tala
Pegeia, Coral Bay, Pafos Bird & Animal Park
Tombs of the Kings
Pafos Archaeological Park
PINELOPIS DELTA
EFXEINOU PONTOU
NEAS SYNOIKIAS
KUBILAY
SINASI
MOREOU
THERMOPYLON
ATHINAS
SOKRATOUS
LEOFOROS EVAGORA PALLIKARIDI
VASILEOS KONSTANTINOU I
LEOFOROS ELEFTHERIOU VENIZ ELOU
GEORG KANNIGKOS
LEOFOROS NIKOLAOU NIKOLAIDI
ALEXANDROUPOLEOS
KINYRA
AMPELOKIPON
TAFON TON VASILEON
ARISTARCHOU
ICHSAN ALI
KATO PERVOLION
Playing Field
Archaeological Museum
Botanical Garden
Municipal Gardens
Municipal Gardens
LEOFOROS GEORGIOU GRIVA DIGENI
ALEXANDROU PAPAGOU
PYRAMOU
ADAMANTIOU KORAI
Ethnographical Museum
PAFOS
EXO VRYSIS
GIANNOU KRANIDIOTI
TILEMACHOU
Cyprus Handicraft Centre
LEOFOROS APOSTOLOU PAVLOU
PTOLEMAIDOS
PRIAMOU
AGAPINOROS
SOTIRAKI MARKIDI
GEORGIOU X. IOANNIDI
AGION ANARGYRON
Pafos Archaeological Park
Agia Solomoni Catacomb
PLOUTARCHOU
Odeon
Mosaics of Pafos
Saranta Kolones
St Paul's Pillar
KATO PAFOS
Pafos Aquarium
Limnarka
LEOFOROS EVROPIS
POSEIDONOS
IASONOS
SPYROU KYPRIANOU
Entrance to Pafos Archaeological Park
Harbour
Municipal Gardens
Pafos Fort
KLEIOUS
ERATOUS
POSEIDONOS
Mediterranean Sea
Geroskipou
N

i ......Information
...Police Station
..............Airport
.......Bus Station
...........Hospital
.......Post Office

Pafos

0 500 metres
0 500 yards

Pafos (Paphos)

Pafos has seen lots of development in the last few years. The lower town – Kato Pafos – has no shortage of eating and nightlife venues. Upper Pafos, known as Ktima, is more traditionally Cypriot. The town is a listed UNESCO World Heritage Site and therefore has a rich collection of historic attractions. Details can be found at the three tourist information offices: ⓐ 3 Gladstonos Street ⓣ 26 93 28 41; ⓐ 63 Leoforos Poseidonos, Kato Pafos ⓣ 26 93 05 21; and at Pafos Airport ⓣ 26 42 31 61.

BEACHES

There are several small beaches on the seafront along Poseidonos Avenue, and bigger ones a short distance southeast of town at Geroskipou. One of the best beaches in the area is at Coral Bay, 9.5 km (6 miles) north of Pafos and connected by a regular bus service.

THINGS TO SEE & DO

Agia Solomoni Catacomb

This gloomy underground cavern was a refuge for persecuted Christians in ancient times. Local people believe that the tree beside the entrance, festooned with colourful votive cloths, is holy and can cure illness.
ⓐ Leoforos Agiou Pavlou, Kato Pafos ⓛ Open permanently
ⓘ Admission free

Agios Neofytos Monastery

This shrine to the 12th-century Cypriot hermit St Neofytos, who carved a sanctuary (*egkleistra*) into the cliffside, is a popular place of pilgrimage. You can climb a stairway to see a small church in a cave that is decorated with murals.
ⓐ Near Tala village, north of Pafos ⓛ 09.00–12.00, 14.00–16.00 (Apr–Oct); 09.00–16.00 (Nov–Mar) ⓘ Admission charge

Archaeological Museum

In this museum you can view finds from the many local historical sites, such as the Tombs of the Kings. These include pottery, sculpture, coins and jewellery. A set of clay hot-water bottles shows that the ancient Romans found Cyprus chilly in winter.

ⓐ Leoforos Georgiou Griva Digeni ⓣ 26 30 62 15 ⓛ 09.00–17.00 Mon–Fri, 10.00–13.00 Sat, closed Sun ⓘ Admission charge

Ethnographical Museum

This museum contains pieces ranging from Neolithic tools and ancient funerary sculptures, to traditional local costumes and everyday household objects.

ⓐ 1 Exo Vrysis Street ⓣ 26 93 20 10 ⓛ 09.00–17.00 Mon–Sat, 10.00–13.00 Sun ⓘ Admission charge

Geroskipou

This village southeast of Pafos has a long association with the myth of Aphrodite, the Greek goddess of love, as this is where she was said to have had her secret garden. In later times it became a silk-making centre of the Byzantine Empire after Orthodox monks smuggled some silkworms out of China. Now a busy suburb of Pafos, it is noted for a slew of pottery workshops along the main street, and shops selling Cypriot Delight (more commonly known in other countries as Turkish Delight). Geroskipou's tourist district runs along the seafront from Pafos, and is really an extension of the bigger town's hotels and beach zone. There's also a Museum of Folk Art and the Agia Paraskevi Byzantine church.

Odeon

Ruins of Pafos's Greek theatre from the 2nd century AD are sited at the heart of an archaeological zone that includes the not easily recognisable remains of the ancient city's *agora* (marketplace) and a temple to Asklepios, the god of healing.

ⓛ 08.00–17.00 (until 19.30 in summer) ⓘ Admission free (except during the Kourion Drama Festival – see page 78)

Roman mosaics at Pafos

Pafos Aquarium

With lots of display tanks, the aquarium puts on a fine underwater show of marine life from the world's oceans and rivers. Stars of the display are sharks, crocodiles and piranhas, but less dangerous and more colourful creatures also have a place.

Artemidos I, Kato Pafos 26 95 39 20 10.00–20.00 (summer); 09.00–18.00 (winter) Admission charge

Pafos Archaeological Park

Located in a cluster of buildings dating from the Roman period, these mosaics are a UNESCO-listed treasure. The House of Dionysos has scenes from pagan mythology; the House of Orpheus has a mosaic showing Orpheus playing his lyre; the Villa of Theseus is named after a mosaic showing Theseus battling with the Minotaur, and may have been the Roman governor's palace; and the House of Aion has superb mosaics of Greek deities.

Pafos harbour 26 30 62 17 08.00–17.00 (until 19.30 in summer) Admission charge

SHOPPING

The upper town, Ktima, has the best shopping although there are plenty of souvenir shops in Kato Pafos.

Athos Diamond Centre This is certainly one of the best jewellery shops in Pafos, with a big selection, good quality, reasonable prices and helpful staff. ⓐ 79–80 Lighthouse Court, Leoforos Poseidonos, Kato Pafos ⓣ 26 81 16 30

Cyprus Handicraft Centre A branch of this government-operated foundation. ⓐ 64 Leoforos Apostolou Pavlou ⓣ 26 30 62 43

Market Pafos market is small but makes up for this in atmosphere and bustle, and is surrounded by a shopping area. This is the place for souvenirs, lace and leather goods, as well as for fruit and vegetables and fresh seafood. ⓐ Junction of Nikodimou Mylona Street with Leoforos Archiepiskopou Makariou III ⓗ 08.00–13.00 Mon–Sat

Marks & Spencer Focuses on clothes in contrast to the wider range found in Britain, but the goods are of the usual high quality. ⓐ Nikodimou Mylona Street ⓣ 26 22 27 71

Moufflon Bookshop One of the best bookshops for English and international books. ⓐ 30 Kinyras Street ⓣ 26 93 48 50

Debenhams A well-known department store chain with an upmarket selection of goods, but prices are keen and the store is popular. Best buys include clothes, cosmetics, food and ceramic souvenirs. ⓐ Debenhams Kinyras, Ledra Street, Kato Pafos ⓣ 26 94 71 22 ⓐ Debenhams Korivos, Leoforos Dimokratia 2, near Geroskipou ⓣ 26 84 08 40

Pafos Bird and Animal Park

Enjoy all the magic of nature in this unique collection of birds and animals, with daily parrot and owl shows and a children's petting zoo. This park is set among lakes, ponds and gardens and there are free transfers daily (except Friday).

ⓐ St George, Pegeia ⓛ 09.00–17.00 Oct–Mar, 09.00–sunset Apr–Sept
ⓘ Admission charge

Pafos Fort

Built by the Ottomans, this fort stands on the harbour wall, on the site of earlier castles dating back to ancient times.

ⓐ Pafos harbour ⓛ 10.00–18.00 (summer); 10.00–17.00 (winter)
ⓘ Admission charge

Pafos harbour

Filled with colourful fishing boats and tour boats, the pedestrianised harbour is lined with tavernas that – although not the best in Pafos – are popular and atmospheric. You can still see the ancient breakwaters, inside which Greek and Roman vessels once sheltered.

Pegeia

A great dining-out experience is an evening trip to the nearby village of Pegeia, which has a constellation of excellent tavernas with outdoor terraces, all of which offer very good value. Unfortunately, the bus service to Pegeia is minimal even in summer, so it may have to be a car or taxi trip.

St Paul's Pillar

Panagia Chrysopolitissa Church stands on the ruins of an early Christian basilica, containing a pillar where St Paul is said to have been scourged. Nearby Agia Solomoni Catacomb, a mysterious underground chamber, was a refuge for early Christians.

ⓐ Leoforos Agiou Pavlou, Kato Pafos ⓘ The site of St Paul's Pillar is often closed for excavations

Saranta Kolones (Byzantine Castle)

Built during the 12th century on the foundations of an earlier Byzantine fortification, this Crusader-era castle fell down during an earthquake shortly after it was completed.

Ⓐ Saranta Kolonon Street near the harbour Ⓒ Dawn–dusk
Ⓘ Admission free

Snake George Reptile Park

Something a little different for a family outing. Home to more than 100 snakes and other reptiles native to Cyprus.

Ⓐ Near junction of Agios Georgios Road, Pegeia Ⓣ 99 98 76 85
Ⓒ 09.00–17.00 Ⓘ Admission charge

Tombs of the Kings

Dating from the 4th century BC, this is a complex of rock-cut tombs beside the sea, in which the leading citizens of Pafos (rather than kings) were buried. Carved steps lead down to the burial chambers and archaeologists are still uncovering more graves.

Ⓐ Tombs of the Kings (Tafoi ton Vasileon) Road Ⓣ 26 30 62 95
Ⓒ 08.00–19.30 (summer); 08.00–17.00 (winter); 08.00–18.00 (spring and autumn) Ⓘ Admission charge

TAKING A BREAK

Demokritos ££ ❶ Kato Pafos's oldest taverna (dating from 1971) adds traditional Greek and Cypriot dances and live music to its evening menu, making dinner something of a spectacle. The atmosphere is as lively as you would expect and food quality is up there with it. Ⓐ 1 Dionysos Street, Kato Pafos Ⓣ 26 93 33 71

Fettas Corner ££ ❷ One of Pafos's little secrets, a place that Cypriots like to keep for themselves. A back-street location is the somewhat unlikely setting for some of the best Cypriot cooking in town.
Ⓐ 33 Ioannis Agrotis Street Ⓣ 26 93 78 22

Oleastro ££ ❸ A smart restaurant and steakhouse serving Mediterranean specialities, steaks and fish. Large children's menu. ⓐ 58 Poseidonos Avenue ⓣ 26 81 34 56

Cavallini ££–£££ ❹ This is an excellent Italian restaurant with an upmarket approach and fine cooking. The atmosphere is relaxed and friendly. The fettucini in cream sauce with salmon strips is excellent, but there are plenty of other fine dishes to choose from. ⓐ 65 Leoforos Poseidonos (between the Amathous Hotel and Rania Apartments) ⓣ 26 96 41 64

AFTER DARK

Pafos has a good selection of pubs and clubs for evening entertainment. Among the most popular are **Blues Bros Café**, **Bubbles Cocktail Bar** and **California Beach Bar**, all in Agiou Antoniou Street (otherwise known as Bar Street), Kato Pafos. **Boogies** ❺ is a bar-disco that lets visitors provide the live music by way of karaoke. It attracts a mix of local people and tourists. ⓐ Agiou Antoniou Street, Kato Pafos ⓣ 26 94 48 10 ⓛ 21.00–03.00

Hollywood ❻ A good example of a dedicated cocktail bar. No food, no happy hour (all prices are reasonable) and no live music – just cocktails. ⓐ 25 Agiou Antoniou Street, Kato Pafos ⓣ 26 93 13 32

Coral Bay & Pegeia

Coral Bay is simply the best beach between Pafos and Latsi (Latchi), with golden sands and a sheltered bay that is ideal for children. The sun gets fierce here in summer, but you can retreat to the shelter of one of the beach cafés. Pegeia is the main settlement in the area surrounding Coral Bay, connected to it by a growing network of holiday and residential villas. Pegeia's main attraction lies in its old village charm. On the cobbled village square can be seen the Orthodox church and a fountain popularised in Cypriot folk songs.

Beach at Coral Bay

From here you can walk a few kilometres uphill to the Pegeia Forest. The expanding view as you climb the hill is well worth the effort. Afterwards, retire to one of the many excellent village tavernas for lunch or dinner. Sunday lunch is particularly popular with the locals.

THINGS TO SEE & DO

There are ancient ruins on the Maa headland that are worth looking at. Otherwise a walk along the cliffs on either side of Coral Bay, or a stroll among the nearby vineyards, orchards and banana plantations, is the only alternative to the beach. Combined with a visit to a café or bar during the day, and a restaurant in the evening, this makes a pleasant day out from Pafos.

Grivas Boat

This is worth visiting if you are interested in recent Cypriot history. It lies halfway between Pafos and Coral Bay (ask the bus driver to let you off), beside the modern church of Agios Georgios. The Grivas Boat is an old caique, similar to the one in which the Cypriot-born Greek army colonel George Grivas landed, on this spot in 1954, to form EOKA and begin the guerrilla war against British rule.

Watersports

All the sports facilities you could wish for are available at Coral Bay.

EXCURSIONS

Cape Drepano and Agios Georgios

Beside the fishing harbour there is a small beach and a view offshore to tiny Geronisos Island. The cliffs behind the beach are riddled with ancient rock-cut tombs. At their summit stands the modern church of Agios Georgios and a far older chapel of the same name. At the church there is an archaeological site that is worth a visit. 10.00–16.00 Mon–Sat, closed Sun Admission charge

The ancient chapel of Agios Georgios at Cape Drepano

Lara Bay

About 5 km (3 miles) north of Cape Drepano is the Lara Bay Turtle Reserve, a protected beach where Cyprus's endangered green turtles lay their eggs.

TAKING A BREAK

The approach road from Coral Bay to Pegeia is dotted with tavernas and the village centre is home to another cluster of eating places. All have similar menus, offer family cooking and a good atmosphere, and all are great value for money.

Corallo £ A charming taverna serving a huge choice of Cypriot specialities, steaks and fish. ⓐ Coral Bay Road ⓣ 26 62 10 52

Coral King ££ This is the first restaurant on your left as you walk up the hill from Coral Beach into the Coral Bay resort. A wide selection of international and local dishes is available. The décor is smart, and there is indoor and outdoor seating. Also offers a traditional Sunday roast dinner! ⓐ Coral Bay Road ⓣ 26 62 28 50

Peyia Tavern ££ At this restaurant, in the village centre, the owner tells you that *he* is the menu. Grilled meats are his speciality, accompanied by side dishes and washed down by village wine – you pay only for what you drink. ⓐ Pegeia village centre, near the church ⓣ 26 62 10 77

Seriani ££ An attractive, informal restaurant surrounded by trees and plants, and serving a mix of Cypriot dishes, steaks and seafood. Fresh sea bream is the house speciality. Full English breakfast is also served. ⓐ Coral Bay Shopping Centre ⓣ 26 62 15 15

Polis & Latsi (Latchi)

Polis and Latsi are the haunts of 'alternative' tourists as well as being bases for exploring the rugged Akamas Peninsula and the scarcely developed north coast. The pace of life is slower here and there are far fewer discos and nightclubs than you find in bigger resorts.

BEACHES

The best and most accessible beaches are located at Latsi. Those along the north coast, towards Pomos, are usually deserted. The road from Latsi to the **Baths of Aphrodite** has many side-tracks that lead to the sea and small beaches of pebble and shingle. If you are willing to hike, you will also find tiny deserted beaches on the Akamas Peninsula.

THINGS TO SEE & DO

Boat trips

By taking a boat trip from Latsi harbour you can get a close-up view of the beautiful Akamas Peninsula without doing all the sweating that hikers do. You can take a 'barbecue boat', which goes along the coast and allows you to swim in the turquoise waters of the Blue Lagoon while your on-board barbecue is being prepared. There are also glass-bottomed boats, and you can hire your own powerboat to take you into tiny bays that no one else can reach.

Latsi

This is the main seaside resort on the northwestern coast, and, when you see how small Latsi is, it gives a good indication of the kind of tourism that rules in this area. The hotels are mostly small scale and the coast and interior are largely undeveloped – although there are clear signs that this happy state of affairs won't last for ever. Latsi is basically a fishing harbour, surrounded by a slew of excellent seafood restaurants and an adjacent beach. It is also the gateway to the Akamas Peninsula.

Seaside bar, Latsi

Polis

A short distance east of Latsi, Polis is the main town in the area, and a place for shopping and dining out. The centre is attractive and maintains the intimate feel of this part of Cyprus. It stands at the heart of Chrysochou Bay and was the site of the ancient Greek port town of Marion, whose remains lie under the fields hereabouts. The town's main square, Dimarcheiou Plateia, and the surrounding streets form a mostly pedestrians-only zone, with a cluster of good restaurants with pavement terraces, café-bars where you can have a quick snack or a refreshing glass of fresh fruit juice, and shops selling newspapers, souvenirs and clothes. The Polis tourist information office is at ⓐ 2 Vasileos Stasioikou Street ⓣ 26 32 24 68

Polis Archaeological Museum

The museum contains finds from the site of the ancient Greek city of Marion. The city was destroyed in the wars of succession following the death of Alexander the Great, then later rebuilt and renamed Arsinoë. You can see a few of the remains amid orange groves.

ⓐ Leoforos Archiepiskopou Makariou III, Polis, on the edge of town ⓣ 26 32 29 55 ⓗ 08.00–14.00 Mon–Fri (also 15.00–18.00 Thur), 09.00–17.00 Sat (Sept–June); 08.00–14.00 Mon–Fri, 09.00–17.00 Sat (July & Aug) ⓘ Admission charge

Watersports

As well as powerboat hire and diving with PADI instructors, the Latsi Watersports and Diving Centre offers the chance to dive with the green turtles on a water-scooter in a group limited to four people.
ⓐ Latsi main street ⓣ 26 32 20 95

TAKING A BREAK

Archontariki ££ Beautifully served Cypriot and international cuisine is the hallmark of this traditional restaurant. There is also an outside eating garden. ⓐ 14 Leoforos Makarios, Polis ⓣ 26 32 13 28

Old Town ££ This is an attractive garden restaurant with the most extensive menu in Polis. The food is excellent and there are good vegetarian dishes. You can dine outside in the garden shaded by trellised vines. Prawns Santorini and sizzling steak are good choices.
ⓐ Polis–Pafos road ⓣ 26 32 27 58

Periyiali ££ Right on the beachfront, this homely restaurant serves an excellent fish *meze* and wonderful seafood. ⓐ Latsi seafront
ⓣ 26 32 12 88

Psaropoulos ££ The owners of this restaurant come from a family of fishermen, so the freshness of the fish could not be better. Try the octopus and garlic prawns. ⓐ Polis–Latsi road ⓣ 26 32 19 89

Yiangos & Peter ££–£££ This friendly place would be one of the front-runners in any competition for Cyprus's best seafood restaurant.
It has a great position beside Latsi harbour, and gets its fish straight off the boat. The fresh sea bream is excellent, as are the king prawns in garlic butter. ⓐ Latsi harbour ⓣ 26 32 14 11

▶ *Lefkara, famous for its lace*

EXCURSIONS
Out & about

Stavrovouni & Lefkara

The hills west of Larnaka rise up from the coastal plain through an increasingly rugged landscape, before merging with the eastern reaches of the Troodos Mountains in an area called Pitsilia.

Monasteries such as Stavrovouni find a natural home in this isolated country, and some of Cyprus's most unspoiled villages can be seen. One village, Lefkara, has earned an international reputation for its superb handmade lace.

Stavrovouni Monastery

There used to be a shrine to Aphrodite on top of the 610-m (2,000-ft) high rocky outcrop where Stavrovouni now perches, with a view over a desolate landscape all the way to Lefkosia in one direction and to the sea in the other. St Helena, mother of the Roman Emperor Constantine the Great, founded the Mountain of the Cross Monastery in AD 327, endowing it with a piece of the True Cross she had discovered in the Holy Land. Ironically, today's women are allowed no closer than the car park.

Icon artistry Greek Orthodox religious icons that can cost up to several thousand pounds have been produced in the workshops at Stavrovouni Monastery for years. Father Kallinikos, who is renowned and admired throughout the area, has made hundreds of icons in the old Byzantine way using tempera on linen over wood, or, more rarely, liquid wax and oils, sometimes mixed with 23-carat gold leaf. The icons are held in the highest regard by the Orthodox Church.

Stavrovouni has been destroyed and rebuilt many times through the centuries, with its present incarnation dating from the 17th century. The venerated relic of the True Cross hangs beside the iconostasis (altar screen) in the church, covered in gold leaf and set in a silver-ornamented wooden crucifix.

ⓐ Off the Lefkosia–Lemesos road ◷ 08.00–12.00, 15.00–18.00 (summer); 08.00–12.00, 15.00–17.00 (winter) ❶ Admission free; men only; dress respectfully; no cameras

The imposing Stavrovouni Monastery

Lefkara

This is not one village but two – although Kato (Lower) Lefkara and Pano (Upper) Lefkara are only separated by a few hundred metres. Kato Lefkara's pastel-hued houses present a picture of idyllic charm, while Pano Lefkara is busier, with more shops, tavernas and parking places – both of these pretty villages are worth visiting.

Lacemakers In both parts of Lefkara you will see women sitting out of doors, in good weather, painstakingly threading handmade Lefkara lace. Lace has been made in Lefkara for centuries, and Leonardo da Vinci is said to have come here to buy lace for Milan Cathedral. Lefkaran men once travelled abroad for months at a time as sales representatives for this exquisite handiwork, leaving the women at home, stitching. Nowadays they do their selling from the village. Silverware and Turkish (or Cypriot) Delight, known as *loukoumi*, are other Lefkaran specialities.

LACE CREATIONS

In *lefkaritika*, the traditional lacemaking style, no pattern is ever repeated. Mothers pass on their skills to their daughters, and visitors to Lefkara can watch three generations of the same family at work and see the beautiful patterns unfold: geometric motifs, a characteristic zigzag called 'the river' and natural patterns such as butterflies. Some pieces take as long as a year to make.

Royal Chapel of Agia Ekaterina

Some rough-road driving takes you across country on a dusty track from Lefkara via Klavia to Pyrga. Here an Orthodox monk is supervising what seems likely to be a decades-long renovation of the ruined medieval church of Agia Ekaterina. The church is notable not only for its isolated location and scenic outlook, but also in its own right.

Open permanently

Agios Minas

Tucked into a little valley near Kato Drys, the flower-bedecked convent is a typically tranquil religious retreat. The nuns make and sell icons and honey, both of which are noted for their quality.

Open for group visits only, Mon–Fri Dress respectfully

Fikardou

This village, in the Troodos foothills, has a rich folk-architectural heritage. It has been declared a conservation zone to preserve the wooden-balconied houses dating from the Ottoman period, as well as the general rustic charm of this unspoiled Cypriot village.

Gourri

Not far from Fikardou, Gourri also has Ottoman-era houses with carved wooden balconies. Unlike its neighbour, however, it is not an official conservation zone.

Machairas Monastery

The handsome monastic complex commands a magnificently scenic view over the rugged Pitsilia district. Machairas's history goes back to the 12th century, when an icon of the Virgin is said to have been found on the site. The present structure dates from the early 20th century, but the church has managed to hang on to its icon. An EOKA freedom fighter was killed near here by British troops in the 1950s, and his grave has become a place of pilgrimage for Cypriots.

22 35 93 34 Open for group visits only, 09.00–12.00 Mon, Tues & Thur Cameras and videos are not allowed; dress respectfully

The Byzantine Machairas Monastery

The ruined agora *(marketplace) at Amathous*

Cape Kiti & Amathous

The coastline from Larnaka to Lemesos is relatively untouched by tourist development, except in the immediate neighbourhood of the two towns.

Driving from one to the other on the coast road, or inland near the motorway, you will encounter several sites of interest that can be visited independently or on an organised tour.

Choirokoitia Neolithic Village

In the foothills of the Troodos Mountains, the rough foundations of circular homes, which must have looked like big stone beehives, straggle up the steep slopes of a bleak promontory overlooking the Maroni River. They were occupied from the 7th to the 4th centuries BC by Stone Age people who buried their dead in the foetal position under the floors. They also made fertility symbols from conical stones.

24 32 27 10 09.00–19.30 Mon–Fri, 09.00–17.00 Sat & Sun (summer); 09.00–17.00 (winter); 09.00–18.00 (spring & autumn) Admission charge

Kamares Aqueduct

Southwest of Larnaka, between the Lemesos road and the Salt Lake, are the 33 remaining arches of a ruined aqueduct built by the Ottoman Turks in the 18th century to bring water from the foothills of the Troodos to Larnaka.

Larnaka Salt Lake

In winter, the lake bed here fills with shallow, salty water and pink flamingos are among the bird species that flock here to feed. By summer it has dried out to a hard, crystalline sheen and you can walk across it. The salt used to be collected commercially, but pollution from airliners using nearby Larnaka International Airport has made it unfit for human consumption. There is a Christian legend that Lazarus turned the soil to salt when a local woman refused to give him some grapes from her vineyard. A nature trail around the lake connects to the Aphrodite Cultural Route.

Hala Sultan Tekke

This mosque, set in a grove of palm trees on the shore of Larnaka Salt Lake, is famed for its tomb of Hala Sultan (or Umm Haram), a relative of the Prophet Mohammed, who died here in AD 649 during an Arab raid on Cyprus. The stone that protects the sepulchre is covered in green cloths of mourning and is said to have flown miraculously from Mount Sinai in Egypt. Muslim ships sailing within sight of the shrine's domes and minarets used to lower their colours as a mark of respect. The mosque dates from the early 19th century, and the grandmother of the late King Hussein of Jordan is also entombed here.

07.30–19.30 (summer); 09.00–17.00 (winter); 09.00–18.00 (spring and autumn) Admission free; donations welcome

Church of Panagia Angeloktisti

At Kiti village, about 7 km (4 miles) west of Larnaka, Our Lady 'Built by the Angels' was rebuilt in the 11th century on a 5th-century foundation. The semicircular apse is embellished with a 6th-century mosaic of the Virgin and Child accompanied by the Archangels Gabriel and Michael. This is one of only seven Byzantine religious mosaics to survive in the Orthodox world, and the workmanship in its tiny squares of coloured and precious stones is outstanding, bearing comparison with the mosaics of the Byzantine Emperor Justinian and Empress Theodora in the Church of San Vitale in Ravenna, Italy.

08.00–12.00, 14.00–16.00 Visitors must dress respectfully

Kiti Tower

Beside the sea at rugged Cape Kiti, several kilometres from Kiti village, this is a stone watchtower built by the Venetians as part of an early-warning system designed to prevent the invasion of Cyprus by the Turks in the 16th century. A lighthouse stands on steep cliffs close by the sea.

Zygi

This is a small village on an undeveloped stretch of coastline. The day's catch from fishing harbours along the coast ends up on the menus of a line of good fish restaurants along the seafront.

Governor's Beach

A popular beach east of Lemesos – its black sand soaks up the sun's heat. By noon it is scorching hot, so watch out for your bare feet!

Agios Georgios Alamanos Convent

The nuns here sell honey and icons at this tranquil convent near the coast, midway between Governor's Beach and Amathous. A nearby track leads to the sea at a rocky beach.

Daily Admission free

Amathous

Founded by the Phoenicians around 1000 BC, Amathous backed the Persians in the Greek wars, some 500 years later, but changed sides when Alexander the Great came knocking. Such pragmatism perhaps explains why so much survives – as much as England's King Richard the Lionheart saw when he landed at Amathous to attack Cyprus in 1191, on his way to the Crusades. There are the remains of the *acropolis* (hilltop fortress) and the *agora* (marketplace), as well as temples to Aphrodite, Adonis and Hercules. From the later era there are a Roman bath-house, an early Christian basilica and marble columns carved with a complex spiral pattern. The main archaeological site overlooks the sea 11 km (7 miles) east of Lemesos.

09.00–19.30 (summer); 09.00–17.00 (winter); 09.00–18.00 (spring and autumn) Admission charge

The Akrotiri Peninsula

Jutting into the Mediterranean west of Lemesos, the Akrotiri Peninsula is occupied almost entirely by Britain's Akrotiri Sovereign Base Area. Although much of the peninsula is accessible, the military installations around RAF Akrotiri are closed to the public, putting the promontories at Cape Zevgari and Cape Gata out of bounds. Only small-scale commercial activity is allowed, which has preserved the peninsula's natural environment from overdevelopment.

Kourion archaeological site

Kolossi Castle

About 14 km (8½ miles) west of Lemesos, Kolossi Castle was the Grand Commandery of the Knights of the Order of St John of Jerusalem, and later of the Knights Templar, after the Crusaders were driven out of the Holy Land in 1291. The existing structure dates from 1454. A romantic lookout place, with stout walls and turreted battlements, Kolossi withstood sieges by Genoese and Mameluke invaders. In addition to the central keep, there are the remains of a basilica, a sugar factory and an aqueduct. Fleur-de-lys symbols are carved on walls and fireplaces, and the entrance hall of the keep has a mural of the Crucifixion.
25 93 49 07 09.00–19.30 (summer); 09.00–17.00 (winter); 09.00–18.00 (spring and autumn) Admission charge

Kourion Archaeological Museum

Finds from excavations at the nearby archaeological sites of Kourion and the Sanctuary of Apollo Ylatis (see pages 78–9) are displayed here, including pottery, oil-lamps, coins, ornaments, *amphorae* (wine- and oil-storage jars), sculptures and votive offerings. A poignant group of three skeletons – almost certainly a husband, wife and their small child – huddle together as fate left them when they perished in the earthquake that demolished Kourion in AD 365.
25 93 24 53 09.00–14.30 Mon–Fri (also 15.00–17.00 Thur, except July & Aug), closed Sat & Sun Admission charge

Episkopi Barracks

The Royal Air Force base at Akrotiri is one of the two British Sovereign Base Areas in Cyprus (the other is at Dhekelia, near Larnaka). A little piece of Britain beside the Mediterranean, the SBA's Episkopi Barracks is modelled on an English suburb. Inside, the military personnel and their families have their own houses, shops, churches, banks, hospitals and sports facilities such as cricket fields and polo pitches. The coast road from Lemesos to Pafos runs through the barracks.

Akrotiri Salt Lake

Although dried out in summer, the lake is filled with shallow water in winter and is a great place for birdwatchers. You can see pink flamingos, ducks, waders and other species, including the Cyprus warbler, black-winged stilt, chukar, crested lark, marsh sandpiper, broad-billed sandpiper, egret, heron and little ringed plover. The flamingos feed on small crustaceans that flourish in the salty water. In summer, the glittering salt lake looks as if it has a solid surface, but do not try to cross it on foot, by bike or in a vehicle – it isn't as firm as it looks.

Agios Nikolaos ton Gaton

The monastery of St Nicholas of the Cats is so called because of the cats supposedly introduced to Cyprus in the 4th century by St Helena, the mother of the Roman Emperor Constantine the Great, to rid the island of poisonous snakes. There are still plenty of cats at Agios Nikolaos, basking in the glow of their forefathers' victory, watched over by the nuns. The original monastery was founded during Constantine's reign (AD 324–37), but the present structure comprises the restored remnants of a 13th-century abbey abandoned when the Ottoman Turks invaded Cyprus in 1570.
Daily Admission free

Lady's Mile Beach

This long, sandy and – usually – deserted stretch of beach lies just outside Lemesos and is named after the place where the wife of a British officer walked her horse during the colonial period. Frequent strong winds make the waters here an excellent arena for windsurfing. Its major drawback is the unsightly view across to the harbour installations at Lemesos.

Fassouri plantations

A green area of citrus groves has been established around the village of Fassouri, west of Lemesos. You can drive or cycle around the orchards on roads shaded from the sun by cypress trees, while breathing in air scented with the tang of oranges, lemons and grapefruit.

Kolossi Castle

Boat trip

A trip around Akrotiri Peninsula can be made by excursion boat from Lemesos. Leaving the fishing harbour, you pass the busy commercial port, with its constant stream of cargo ships coming and going. From there you cruise past sandy Lady's Mile Beach on the eastern shore of the peninsula, with the salt lake visible behind. RAF Akrotiri lies out of sight behind a screen of sand dunes and vegetation.

Rounding Cape Gata, then Cape Zevgari, you sail along the western shore, then get a spectacular view of the cliffside at Kourion, on which the ruins of the ancient city stand. There are frequent excursions from Lemesos fishing harbour.

Kourion

Spend a few hours in the world of the ancient Greeks and Romans at the dramatic clifftop city of Kourion, overlooking the sea, and further along the coast at the well-preserved Sanctuary of Apollon Ylatis. When you add in famous historic sites and the attractive seaside resort of Pissouri Beach, the experience combines into a memorable day out.

Kourion (Curium)

The ruins of the ancient city are perched on a clifftop overlooking the sea 19 km (12 miles) west of Lemesos. Kourion was founded by Greek colonists in the 14th century BC. It was an important city-state throughout Cyprus's early history and reached its peak of influence under the Romans. It was destroyed by an earthquake in AD 365, rebuilt and finally abandoned after Arab raids in the 7th century.
25 93 42 50 08.00–19.30 (summer); 08.00–17.00 (winter); 08.00–18.00 (spring and autumn) Admission charge

Theatre and mosaics

There are three main parts to the site. The first includes the Odeon, a magnificent Graeco-Roman theatre, built into the cliff face and with a stunning view. Visitors pose theatrically for snapshots on the stage, one of the great sites of the ancient world. Beside it is the House of Eustolios, a private Roman villa dating from the 4th century AD. One of its mosaics shows a young woman who symbolises the Creation.

In the second part of the site is an early Christian basilica, a 5th-century church overlooking the sea. The nearby Roman forum is still being excavated. In this zone is a Roman water reservoir. A residential area flanking the forum has a number of buildings containing fine mosaics, including those in the House of the Gladiators and the House of Achilles.

Located 2 km (1 mile) west of the main site, the city's stadium, dating from the 2nd century AD, was an arena for track and field sports. Not much remains, apart from the lower reaches of its wall.
Open permanently Admission included in entry price for main site

Ruins at Kourion

Kourion Drama Festival

In summer, the Odeon at Kourion features performances of plays by ancient Greek writers, Shakespeare and modern dramatists, as well as classical and modern music, ballet performances and sound-and-light shows. Check with the tourist office for programme details.

Sanctuary of Apollon Ylatis

About 3 km (2 miles) west of Kourion are the remains of the Sanctuary of Apollon Ylatis, an important temple and place of pilgrimage in ancient times. Dormitories and halls can be clearly seen, along with an exercise court, a baths complex and the Priest of Apollo's house.

At the heart of the sanctuary is the partially restored Temple of Apollo. Any visitors sacrilegious enough to touch the altar of Apollo were thrown into the sea from the nearest headland – so be careful!

25 99 10 49 09.00–19.30 (summer); 09.00–17.00 (winter); 09.00–18.00 (spring and autumn) Admission charge

Pissouri & Kouklia

The wild and scenic coastline – stretching from the ancient city of Kourion to the Rock of Aphrodite about midway between Lemesos and Pafos – is worth seeing just for its own beauty.

Kouklia

This village is the site of Palaia Pafos, sometimes known as Palea Pafos meaning Old Pafos, one of ancient Cyprus's most important city states. On a hill outside Kouklia, archaeologists have excavated part of the city walls, uncovering a siege mound and counter-tunnels dating from the Cypriot rebellion against Persia in 498 BC. Despite indications of fierce resistance, the rebel city was eventually captured.

Sanctuary of Aphrodite

This World Heritage shrine to the Greek goddess of love was renowned throughout the ancient Mediterranean. You can see the ruins of the first sanctuary dating back to the 2nd and 1st centuries BC and later Roman temple ruins from the 1st century AD.

The on-site museum is housed in an Ottoman-era farm, called the Chiftlik, and displays finds from the Sanctuary, including a conical stone that may have been an archaic cult idol of Aphrodite, clay pots and a variety of figurines.

ⓐ Kouklia village ⓣ 26 43 21 55 ◷ 08.00–16.00
ⓘ Admission charge

Rock of Aphrodite (Petra tou Romiou)

This unusual rock formation, standing in shallow sea water beside the Lemesos–Pafos road, must be the most famous spot in Cyprus. This is where Aphrodite, goddess of beauty and love, was born, wafted ashore on a seashell, to be met by her handmaidens, the Hours, who decked her out with precious jewels, set a crown of gold on her head, and gave her earrings of gold and copper. Aphrodite's Rock is a favourite spot for romantic couples, particularly at sunset.

Grey skies over pillars of the Sanctuary of Aphrodite

UNKINDEST CUT

According to the ancient Greek writer Hesiod, the white foam from which Aphrodite arose came from the genitals of Uranos, which had been severed by his son Kronos and cast into the sea. In reality – if the term can be applied to mythology – she was possibly imported from the Near East as a fertility goddess.

The beach is reached via a tunnel under the busy coast road from the Cyprus Tourism Organisation car park and rest area Open permanently

Pissouri Beach

Reached via a side-road off the Lemesos–Pafos road, Pissouri's beach offers a selection of tavernas and shops, but remains one of Cyprus's quieter resorts.

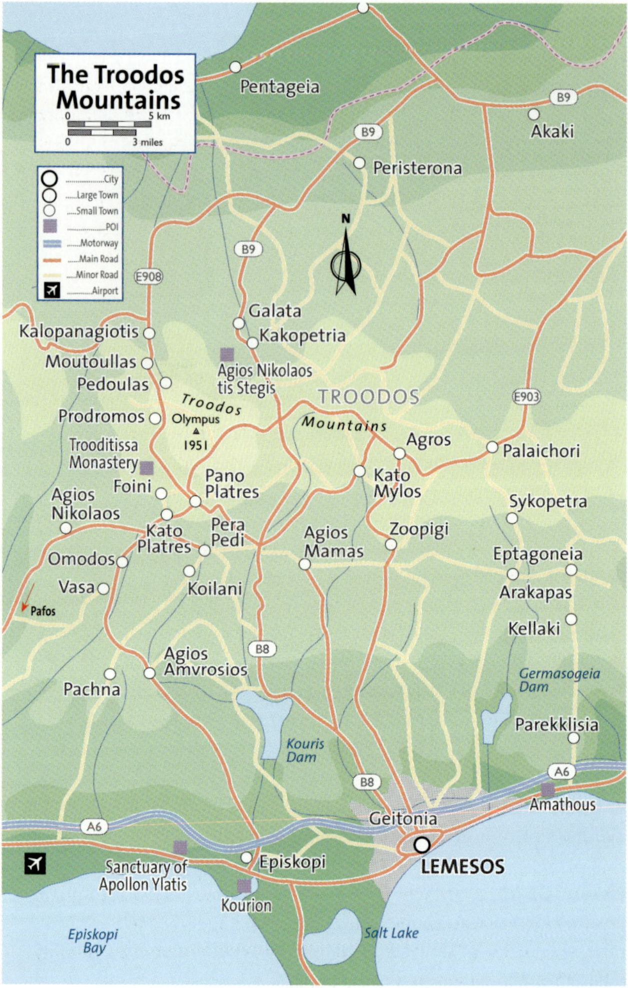

The Troodos Mountains

0 5 km
0 3 miles

City
Large Town
Small Town
POI
Motorway
Main Road
Minor Road
Airport

Pentageia
B9
Akaki
B9
Peristerona
N
B9
E908
Galata
Kakopetria
Kalopanagiotis
Moutoullas
Agios Nikolaos tis Stegis
Pedoulas
TROODOS
E903
Troodos
Olympus
1951
Mountains
Prodromos
Agros
Palaichori
Trooditissa Monastery
Kato Mylos
Pano Platres
Foini
Agios Nikolaos
Sykopetra
Pera Pedi
Kato Platres
Agios Mamas
Zoopigi
Omodos
Eptagoneia
Vasa
Koilani
Arakapas
Pafos
Kellaki
B8
Agios Amvrosios
Germasogeia Dam
Pachna
Parekklisia
Kouris Dam
A6
B8
Amathous
Geitonia
A6
LEMESOS
Episkopi
Sanctuary of Apollon Ylatis
Kourion
Salt Lake
Episkopi Bay

The Troodos Mountains

In summer the cool air of the Troodos Mountains, scented with eucalyptus and pine, is an irresistible draw for many otherwise beach-bound tourists. There are nature reserves, walking and cycling trails and forest stations to explore, as well as Byzantine-era monasteries. If you are fit and feeling slightly adventurous, a wonderful way to see the mountains is from the saddle of a mountain bike, for hire in Plano Platres and Kakopetria.

THE ROUTE

Pafos and Lemesos are the resorts closest to the Troodos Mountains. This day-trip itinerary begins in Pafos, snakes its way through many of the mountains' stellar sights, then rolls downhill to end in Lemesos. You can easily do the route in reverse, beginning in Lemesos and ending in Pafos. In either case, you return to your home base on the A6 motorway, which runs from Lemesos to Pafos.

Take the Lemesos road from Pafos, through Geroskipou and past Pafos Airport, to Kouklia, where you turn left, passing the big Asprokremmos Dam. At Nikokleia village, you have a choice; you can either take the lower road, to the right, along the Diarizos river valley, or opt for the higher road, to the left, which follows the ridgeline for part of the way, looking down into the neighbouring valley of the Xeros Potamos river. Both routes are scenic, and both bring you out near Filousa village, where you follow signs for **Agios Nikolaos** and Pano Platres, for a refreshment break.

Pano Platres

The main mountain resort, Pano Platres, and its neighbouring Kato Platres are as popular in summer as they are during the winter skiing season. The Troodos Mountains tourist office is here, in Village Square, providing maps and booklets on signposted mountain trails ✆ 25 42 13 16. Tumbling 18 m (60 ft), Kaledonia Falls near Plano Platres are fed by a perennial stream, the Kryos.

The 2-km (1-mile) long Kaledonia Trail follows a route through the forest to the falls from near Troodos village. Continue uphill through Pano Platres, passing a trout farm and the pathway to Kaledonia Falls outside town. Follow the winding road up through the mountains to Troodos – the President of Cyprus's summer residence is somewhere off to your right, out of sight among the trees.

Troodos

Troodos village, near the roof of the mountains, has gift shops, tavernas and car parks, and makes a bustling change from the loneliness of the mountain trails. Go right at the crossroads in Troodos, passing the disused asbestos mine at Pano Amiantos and the desolate scenery it has left on the mountainside, and descend the northern slopes of the mountains, towards Kakopetria.

Kakopetria

Kakopetria is a fast-growing resort on the northern edge of the mountains but close enough to make a convenient base for exploring them. Its old village centre is being preserved. Located here is **The Mill Hotel** (see page 87), a tall, wooden-built place, overlooking a mountain stream. Continue downhill a short way to Galata.

Galata

Galata is a handsome village of white-painted houses at the head of the fertile Solea Valley. It has a small **Folk Art Museum** and a restored Ottoman inn. Two old churches just outside the village are on UNESCO's list of World Cultural Heritage Sites for their superb religious frescoes: **Panagia Podythou Church** and the nearby timber-roofed **Church of Archangelos Michail**. Return to Galata, and make a short detour to the right, to Agios Nikolaos tis Stegis.

Agios Nikolaos tis Stegis

This 11th-century Byzantine church with two roofs, the outer being a protection against snow, is a UNESCO World Cultural Heritage Site,

Agios Nikolaos tis Stegis, Kakopetria

thanks to an interior that is decorated with religious frescoes. Its scenic location probably has as much to do with attracting visitors, however. You now have to return to Troodos, and turn right at the village crossroads, to Mount Olympus.

Mount Olympus

The Troodos Mountains rise up to the peak of Mount Olympus, which is 1,952 m (6,404 ft) high. In winter you can ski the snows of Olympus and in summer hike its nature trails. The summit is occupied by the dome of a British military radar station. Continue down the northwestern face of the mountains, past Prodromos Reservoir, to Prodromos.

Prodromos

This is the location of the Cyprus Forestry College, whose graduates play a big part in the effort to restore the island's tree cover. Prodromos stands at an altitude of 1,390 m (4,560 ft) and has a fine view of villages further down the slopes, ironically because it is in an area that has not been heavily forested. Continue downhill to Pedoulas.

Pedoulas

This village in the Marathasa Valley is famous for its cherries. In June, roadside stalls are filled with the dark fruit, piled up in baskets like heaps of precious stones. One of the Troodos Mountains' most popular resorts, Pedoulas has several good restaurants. The village's **Ecclesiastical Museum** 22 95 36 36 and Archangelos Michail Church are worth a visit. Continue downhill to Moutoullas.

Moutoullas

This is an attractive Marathasa Valley village, whose 13th-century Byzantine church of Panagia tou Moutoullas is another UNESCO World Cultural Heritage Site. Continue downhill to Kalopanagiotis.

Kalopanagiotis

Formerly a spa resort thanks to its sulphur springs, nowadays visitors come to see the three side-by-side churches, under a single snow roof, of Agios Ioannis Lampadistis Monastery, a UNESCO World Cultural Heritage Site. Return to Prodromos and take the lower road to Pano Platres, passing Panagia Trooditissa Monastery.

Trooditissa Monastery

Overlooking a steep gorge some 5 km (3 miles) from Pano Platres, rustic Trooditissa (Daily), founded in the 13th century, boasts a priceless silver-gilt icon of the Madonna. Continue to a side road leading off to the right to Foini village.

Village of Pedoulas in the heart of the Troodos Mountains

Foini

A pretty little village with steep streets, clinging to the hillside, Foini is noted for its traditional Cypriot pottery as well as modern ware, and its Folk Art Museum. Take the road through Kato Platres, which puts you on the road to Lemesos.

TAKING A BREAK

Civic £ A restaurant popular with locals, which offers tourists the chance to sample traditional Cypriot dishes. Seating inside and out. International dishes also available. ⓐ Located in Paliometocho village between Troodos and Lefkosia ⓣ 22 83 56 40

The Mill Hotel ££ A popular restaurant noted for its excellent mountain trout, and with a full Cypriot and international menu. ⓐ The Mill Hotel, 8 Milos Street, Kakopetria ⓣ 22 92 25 36 ⓦ www.cymillhotel.com

Troodos wine villages

Spread across the southern and western foothills of the Troodos Mountains are the vineyards from which Cypriot wines are derived. The vineyards remain the key to prosperity and continued existence for many villages here, where life moves at its own pace and rhythm, and thousands of families are involved in grape production. Wine is among Cyprus's most important exports, with Britain its main customer.

Commandaria region

A narrow slice of the southern Troodos wine district is given over to the production of the grapes used to make the distinctive Commandaria dessert wine. Dotted with villas and pretty villages, the region has an ambience similar to that of European wine-producing regions such as Tuscany.

Krassochoria

Off the southwestern edge of the Troodos Mountains is another grape-growing region, the Krassochoria (wine villages), whose villagers are up to their knees in grape juice come autumn – or, at any rate, they would be if the whole process hadn't by now been automated.

THE ROUTE

Beginning and ending in Lemesos, this route leads you through the heart of the district, with spectacular scenery and mountain villages. Leave Lemesos on the A1 motorway east, until junction 21, where you turn off towards Parekklisia. Follow this road north through Kellaki, turn left at Eptagoneia to Arakapas, then right through Sykopetra to Palaichori.

Palaichori

The Byzantine-era village, with its white-painted houses and red-tiled roofs, looks like an avalanche frozen in the act of tumbling down the steep hillside to which it clings. Vineyards (with grapes that produce a fine red wine), orchards, almond trees and vegetable patches form a delightful pastoral background. Leave Palaichori on the Agios Theodoros road and turn right, following the signs for Agros.

Agros

A pretty village that produces rose water, mineral water and wine (not necessarily in that order of preference) as liquid inducements to make a visit. Leave Agros to the south, on the road that runs through Kato Mylos to Zoopigi.

Zoopigi

One of the villages that produces the Commandaria dessert wine, Zoopigi is surrounded by vineyards in a beautifully green area off the southern slopes of the Troodos. It is also an important producer of *zivania* (also called 'Cyprus whisky'), distilled from the skin, pips and other grape bits left over after the wine has been fermented. The alcohol is so strong that Cypriots wisely drink it in moderation.

From Zoopigi continue south a short way to a crossroads and turn right (west), through Agios Mamas, to Pera Pedi, where you go south a short distance to Koilani.

Koilani

A village in the heart of the grape-growing, wine-making district of the southern Troodos, Koilani keeps one foot in heaven's camp with its Ecclesiastical Museum. Housed within the grounds of the village church, the museum's collection includes icons, religious vessels, antique prayer books and ornaments, some of which display fine craftsmanship in silver. Return to Pera Pedi and continue west to Mandria, where you turn south towards Omodos.

Omodos

The largest of the Krassochoria wine villages, Omodos has acted to preserve its traditional character while benefiting from tourism. The village centre has been restored, arts and crafts workshops have been

established, and some residents invite visitors for a guided tour of their traditional homes. In addition, there is a restored 15th-century wine press known as *linos*. A wine festival is held in the village every August.

Among the goods for sale are the local lace, called *pipilla*, and ring-shaped bread, called *arketana*. The restored house interiors are hung with gourds, and kitchen utensils hang beside the traditional wood-fired oven. The houses also have cellars where large earthenware pots, called *pitharia*, formerly filled with wine, are kept.

The **Monastery of Stavros**, in Omodos, has a golden cross containing hemp fibres said to have come from the ropes that bound Jesus to the Cross, and another that is said to contain a fragment of the True Cross. Continue south on the main road, making a short detour outside of town to Vasa.

Vasa

Wine and mineral water are produced and bottled in this red-roofed Krassochoria village near Omodos. Vasa is also renowned for its mineral water, bottled here from the village spring. The house of the noted Cypriot poet Dimitris Lipertis, who died in 1937, has been restored and can be visited. Return to the main road and continue south to Agios Amvrosios.

Agios Amvrosios

'Green' wines are produced from organically grown grapes in this southern Troodos village, at the **Ecological Winery** (t 25 94 39 51 ◷ 08.00–14.00 Mon–Fri) owned by Georgios Yiallouros. The winery produces up to 60,000 bottles of environmentally sound wines a year, which taste quite good. Stay on the main road south, back to Lemesos.

A BITE TO EAT

There are several cafés around the main square in Omodos, but for traditional Cypriot cooking, try the **Ambelothea Restaurant** **££** a Near the hospital t 25 42 13 66

Monastery of Stavros, Omodos

Cruising to Egypt & the Greek Islands

A holiday in Cyprus puts you in easy reach of the wonders of Egypt and the beautiful Greek Islands. The best way to take advantage of this is to enjoy one of the many cruises on offer departing from Lemesos. There are a number of cruise and tour options available.

Getting there

Several companies operate cruises from Cyprus to Egypt and the Greek Islands. Cruises can be booked easily through your holiday representative or the tourist office as well as direct with the cruise lines. You can also readily obtain full information from:

- **Louis Cruise Lines** ⓣ 25 57 00 00 ⓕ 25 57 36 06 ⓦ www.louiscruises.com
- **Salamis Tours** ⓣ 25 86 00 00 ⓕ 25 36 73 74 ⓦ www.salamis-tours.com

While many of the cruises on offer follow similar itineraries, circumstances may cause changes to be introduced at short notice. The descriptions below give some details about what is on offer, but should not be considered as an exact description of the itinerary.

Three-night cruise to Egypt

Depart Lemesos and arrive in Port Said, located at the entrance of the Suez Canal, at around 06.00. After breakfast on board, you disembark and are taken by air-conditioned coach to the ruins of the historic city of Memphis, once the capital of ancient Egypt.

After leaving Memphis, you will visit a Papyrus Institute to see the oldest type of paper in the world being made, and then you'll be taken to see the Pyramids at Giza. The burial chambers of the Egyptian Pharaohs are located surprisingly close to Cairo and offer a wonderful opportunity to view the past – especially the Great Pyramid of Khufu, one of the Seven Wonders of the World, which stands alongside those of Khafre

The Pyramids at Giza

and Menkaure at the Giza Plateau. The visit will also give you the option to see inside the Third Pyramid and/or visit the Sun Boat, which was constructed to take the Pharaoh on journeys in the afterlife. From here you will move on to visit the mysterious Sphinx and its temple before returning to the ship for the night.

The next day you will visit Cairo – the heart of ancient Egyptian civilisation and one of the most fascinating cities in the world. First stop is a visit to the Egyptian Museum, where some of the most stunning splendours of antiquity can be found. Some of the most precious items ever discovered can be admired here, including the treasures from the tomb of Tutankhamen and an extensive collection of jewellery.

After the Museum, you will visit the oldest church in Cairo, the Hanging Church, which contains relics from the early days of Christianity in Egypt. From here, you will be driven to the Citadel of Salah El Din, which houses the world-famous Alabaster Mosque. From high up on the walls of the citadel, you can enjoy a panoramic view of Cairo.

After leaving Cairo, you will be returned to Port Said, where, after embarkation, the ship sails for Lemesos.

Numerous other options are also available for cruises to the region, including trips to Alexandria and Beirut. You can contact one of the cruise lines mentioned on page 92 for further details.

Greek Islands

Select a cruise to the stunning Greek Islands and leave Lemesos for a fascinating voyage exploring the wonders of the Mediterranean.

Highlights of the Greek Islands include the Lindos area of Rhodes, which was established around 3,000 years ago and was one of the most important civilisations of the ancient world. Visit the Temple of Lindian Athena, built in 550 BC and rebuilt in the 3rd century BC in the form that you see it today. St Paul was shipwrecked at Lindos and founded the Rhodia Church, and the bay next to Lindos Acropolis is still known as St Paul's Bay. The island was also occupied by the Knights of St John, who fortified the Acropolis to protect it against invasion from the Saracens. The old Byzantine church dedicated to the Holy Mother can still be seen inside the Acropolis.

On the island of Kos, visit the Asklepion, which was built in the 4th century BC and dedicated to Hippocrates, father of modern medicine. Due to the sloping terrain, the sanctuary is constructed on three terraces and joined by a magnificent staircase. The first level, the Courtyard of the Temple, was used for various ceremonies and festivals, while the second level is the Great Altar of the Temple. The third level is the Doric Temple of Asklepios, dating from the 2nd century.

A number of cruises are available to the Greek Islands. You should check with the tour operators for destinations, itineraries and prices either before you leave or once you arrive in Cyprus.

The harbour area at Pafos

LIFESTYLE
Island life

Food & drink

Cypriots are rarely happier than when piling convivially into the heaped-up contents of as many food platters as will set a table groaning, but not quite collapsing. You should join them as often as possible, eating out at least several times a week at a traditional taverna. Don't lock yourself up in the hotel restaurant eating 'international' food. Get out, trust your nose and follow wherever it leads.

CYPRIOT FOOD

Your best guide, if you want to taste the genuine flavour of Cypriot food, is to see where the locals go, and go with them. Eating out in Cyprus is a social event, and traditional Cypriot cuisine lends itself to the experience. *Meze* is the best introduction – a torrent of little dishes that arrive on the table in a seemingly endless flood.

Cyprus stands at the crossroads of three continents (Africa, Europe and Asia), and it has absorbed culinary influences from all three. Ordering a *meze* enables you to sample the results in the form of some 20 to 30 dishes, ranging from dips and raw vegetables to fish and meat in richly flavoured sauces. Such a meal is a test of appetite and endurance, which may be why Cypriots linger so long over their meals.

Among many *meze* items are: *haloumi* – a cheese made from the milk of thyme-fed goats, often served grilled; *dolmadakia* – vine leaves stuffed with rice and meat; *lountza* – smoked pork, marinated in red wine; *tahini* – a sesame-seed dip mixed with lemon, garlic and parsley; and *houmous* – a dip made from chickpeas and olive oil.

Main dishes include such favourites as *afelia* – chunks of pork stewed in a red-wine sauce sprinkled with coriander; *souvlakia* – lamb or pork grilled on a skewer; *keftedes* – fried meatballs; *moussaka* – a layered dish of aubergines, potato and minced meat in a béchamel sauce; and *kleftiko* – lamb roasted in an earthenware oven.

BRITISH

As the British make up the single biggest group of foreign visitors to Cyprus, no major resort is without its line-up of traditional British favourites: fish and chips, mushy peas, black pudding, roast beef and the full English breakfast. Pub grub has its place, too. As in Britain, you can also find a more considered interpretation of British cuisine, with fresh ingredients, home baking, regional specialities and vegetarian food.

INTERNATIONAL

Among the German restaurants and bars serving *currywurst* (curry sausage), grilled meats and marvellous German beers, and the

Ordering a meze *is a good way to sample the local food*

Scandinavian restaurants, with their *smorgasbords* and smoked salmon, you will also find Russian restaurants catering for the large number of Russian visitors. Italian and Mexican-style restaurants are popular, as is American-inspired fast food, including McDonald's and Pizza Hut.

WINE

Cypriot wines run the gamut from light and sparkling to full-bodied red, with most popular attention being focused on the light and fruity whites. Commandaria, a sweet red dessert wine with a history dating back to ancient times, is one of Cyprus's most notable products.

Cyprus produces many fine local wines

VAKHIS

If you want to taste authentic Cypriot cuisine, look for a restaurant with the Vakhis certificate. To qualify for the award, restaurants have to use traditional foods and cooking methods and meet criteria set by the Cyprus Tourism Organisation and Higher Hotel Institute. Restaurants include Lofou, Kamares and Kazani in Lofu, Agia Anna in Agia Anna, Mesostrato in Kakopetria, Kinyras in Pafos, Mandra and Voreas in Oroklini, Gonia Tou Anastasi in Tseri and Takis Tavern in Vouni

Good yet inexpensive wines are plentiful. The Ecological Winery at Agios Amvrosios produces wines from organically grown grapes. Panagia Chrysorrogiatissa monastery, near Pano Panagia, has won respect for its high-quality Monte Royia wines. In a taverna, you can't go far wrong if you ask for either the red or white house wine – it will usually have come from some small village vineyard and will be perfectly acceptable.

OTHER DRINKS

Carlsberg has a brewery in Cyprus, and the local KEO and LEON lagers are every bit as good. English beers are a 'speciality' of British pubs on the island. In some bars you will find international beers as well. Cypriot brandy is cheaper and lighter than the French version, and is the main ingredient of 'Brandy Sour', Cyprus's own cocktail.

Menu decoder

Here are some of the authentically Greek-Cypriot dishes that you might encounter in tavernas or pastry shops.

Afelia Pieces of pork soaked in wine and sautéed with oil and coriander

Baklava A sweet pastry popular throughout the Middle East made with finely chopped nuts, honey and filo pastry

Dolmadákia Vine leaves stuffed with rice, onions, dill, parsley, mint and lemon juice

Domátes/piperiés yemistés Tomatoes/peppers stuffed with herb-flavoured rice (and sometimes minced lamb or beef)

Fasólia saláta White beans (haricot, butter beans) dressed with olive oil, lemon juice, parsley, onions, olives and tomato

Kadaifi A sweet pastry with shredded wheat, nuts and honey syrup

Kattimeria These are thin semolina paste delicacies filled with meat and almonds or eggs and cheese

Makaronópitta A pie made from macaroni blended with beaten eggs, cheese and milk, baked in puff pastry

Melitzanosalátta Dip made from baked aubergines, liquidised with tomatoes, onions and lemon juice

Meze A rich selection of appetizers and savouries in up to 20 saucerlike dishes. Various cheeses, like halloumi, kaskavalli or feta. Tomatoes, olives, celery, cucumber, sliced artichokes or smoked ham, houmous, octopus, shrimps, fresh fish, such as barbouni (the delicious red mullet), succulent pieces of chicken, to local titbits such as seftalia (homemade sausage) and koupepia (stuffed vine leaves)

Moussakás Moussaka, made from fried slices of aubergines, interlayered with minced beef and béchamel sauce

Pastíccio Layers of macaroni, *haloumi* cheese and minced meat (cooked with onions, tomatoes and basil), topped with béchamel sauce and baked

Pítta me kymá Meat pie made from minced lamb and eggs, flavoured with onions and cinnamon and baked in filo pastry

Souvlákia Kebab – usually of pork cooked over charcoal

Souzoukko A favourite at Cypriot festivals – it is made by dipping strings of nuts in heated grape juice until it solidifies

Spanakopítta Cigar-shaped pies made from feta cheese, eggs, spinach, onions and nutmeg in filo pastry

Taramosaláta Cod's roe dip made from puréed potatoes, smoked cod's roe, oil, lemon juice and onion

Tyropitákia Small triangular cheese pies made from feta cheese and eggs in filo pastry

Tzatzíki Grated cucumber and garlic in a dressing of yoghurt, olive oil and vinegar

Sample some typical Greek-Cypriot food in the sunshine

Shopping

CYPRUS HANDICRAFT SERVICE

The government-operated Cyprus Handicraft Service (CHS) is a key part of the drive to retain the island's traditional arts and crafts. All of these are under serious threat as children no longer learn the old skills from their parents, and the villages that were the source of many traditional practices are abandoned in favour of the modern towns and resorts. CHS operates a centre in Lefkosia that provides teaching and practical experience, and it has shops in Lefkosia, Larnaka, Lemesos and Pafos. It produces a limited range of well-made items in all kinds of traditional crafts – pottery, embroidery, woodwork, metalwork and so on (see page 23).

ICONS

Greek Orthodox religious icons are painted and sold at many monasteries and convents, and local priests may also try their hand at producing them. Most are simple items, but others are superb pieces of art in demand around the world. Among the latter are those produced at Stavrovouni Monastery, which can cost up to several thousand pounds each (see page 66).

LACE

Lace has been made in Lefkara for centuries in the traditional style called *lefkaritika*, each piece being a unique creation of the village women who sit outdoors in good weather, hand-stitching intricate designs on to pieces of Irish linen. The lace can most easily be bought in Lefkara itself, with the added attraction of seeing how it is made, but it can also be bought at shops and markets elsewhere (see page 67).

LOOM EMBROIDERY

There are several traditional styles of woven cloth. Pafos is noted for *paphitika*, bright geometric designs woven into cloths, cushion covers, bedspreads, curtains, tablecloths and other domestic items. Then

Byzantine icon painting

there are *lefkonika* – towels, aprons and place-mats – and *alatjia*, a silky-smooth striped cotton. Silk takes the limelight at Geroskipou village, near Pafos, which is noted for this material.

POTTERY

The resurgence of craft work in pottery and ceramics means that some sophisticated jugs, bowls and other objects are now being produced. You can find these in good souvenir shops, as well as in market areas of the main towns. One of the best craft potters is the **Lemba Pottery** (t 26 27 08 22), at Lemba village near Pafos.

Traditional pottery is also made at Koloni, Foini (Phini) and Geroskipou. Huge hand-thrown *pitharia* pots, from Kornos, were once used for storing olive oil and wine. They can still be seen, but are now more likely to be filled with flowers. Lapithos village, in what is now the Turkish-occupied part of Cyprus, became known for its porcelain cats, a tradition that was popularised by the British in pre-independence days. Nowadays, Lapithos porcelain cats are produced in the South.

Splashing about at WaterWorld WaterPark

Children

AGIA NAPA

This resort is well supplied with facilities for keeping demanding little consumers amused. There are kamikaze slides, river tube rides and rolling logs at WaterWorld WaterPark (page 30). Dinosaur Park (page 29) has models of prehistoric creatures, complete with sounds. The Thalassa Municipal Museum of Marine Life showcases the wide variety of marine life around Cyprus's coast (pages 29–30).

AKAMAS PENINSULA

Monk seals can be seen off the Akamas Peninsula (page 62) and some 168 bird species and 55 butterfly species have been identified on it, as well as 600 or more plant varieties, so it could be good for a 'nature studies' walk.

AKROTIRI PENINSULA

The Salt Lake (page 76) dries out to a muddy salt flat in summer and in winter its shallow waters are visited by pink flamingos. Nearby Kolossi Castle (page 75) was once the base of the Knights Templar, so it's a great place for pretending to be a gallant knight or a distressed maiden.

LEMESOS

How about making black sandcastles? Governor's Beach (page 73), east of Lemesos, has the black sand you need as a raw material. Lemesos's small zoo is in the Municipal Gardens.

PAFOS

See exotic toucans, eagles, giraffes and reptiles, plus parrot, owl and seal shows daily, at Pafos Bird and Animal Park (page 55). Free transfers from main resorts.

Sports & activities

GOLF

Cyprus is not a noted golfing destination, but it is trying to remedy that situation and now has three good golf courses in the Pafos area. Combined with sunshine they certainly make a worthwhile outing for golfers.

- **Aphrodite Hills Golf and Leisure Centre** – 18 holes, par 71 ⓣ 26 81 87 00
- **Secret Valley Golf Club** – 18 holes, par 71 ⓣ 26 64 27 74
- **Tsada Golf Club** – 18 holes, par 72 ⓣ 26 64 27 74

Mountain biking in the Troodos Mountains

HIKING

There are many hiking and nature trails in Cyprus. Serious hikers will want to plan their own routes into the Troodos Mountains, the Akamas Peninsula or rugged areas around the resorts. Even if all you want to do is a little energetic walking while getting close to nature, but without the paraphernalia of maps, compasses and specialised equipment, there are still plenty of possibilities.

Four signposted nature trails have been established in the Troodos Mountains around Mount Olympus. These are the Artemis, Atalanta, Kalidonia and Persephone trails. In the Akamas Peninsula there are two: the Aphrodite and Adonis. In addition, numerous forest trails have been marked out by the Forestry Department. Further information is available from tourist offices.

MOUNTAIN BIKING

You need a basic level of fitness and cycling skill before trying this seriously, but there are some great mountain-biking areas in Cyprus. If it's real mountains you want, just head for the Troodos Mountains and you will get all the action you can handle.

SKIING

Only in winter, of course! There are two ski lifts and four runs in the Troodos Mountains at Mount Olympus. Skiing is usually – though not always – possible from the beginning of January to the end of March, with ski and boot hire available. **Cyprus Ski Club** ⓐ PO Box 22185, 1518 Lefkosia ⓣ 22 67 53 40 ⓒ 09.00–13.00

WATERSPORTS

All resorts have diving schools with trained professional instructors where you can learn the underwater ropes or go on diving excursions, and, if you are more experienced, get close to the colourful marine life. Windsurfing, kite-surfing and jet-skis are widely available.

Festivals & events

JANUARY

New Year's Day

It is on this day, rather than Christmas Day, that Cypriots exchange seasonal gifts.

FEBRUARY OR MARCH

Carnival

The first day of Lent (50 days before the Orthodox Easter) is known as Green Monday and is the start of the Lenten fast, during which no meat is eaten. In the week before Green Monday, carnivals are held in several towns and villages. The biggest and most colourful is Lemesos's, followed by those of Pafos and Larnaka.

Crazy costumes at the Carnival in Lemesos

MARCH OR APRIL

Easter

On Easter Saturday, bonfires are lit in the evening, on to which effigies of Judas are thrown. Easter Sunday is celebrated by feasting and the breaking of eggs. Easter is the most important religious event of the year.

MAY

Anthesteria

These flower festivals are held at Pafos, Lemesos and several other towns in May to celebrate spring's return, marked with parades and re-enactments of Greek myths.

Kataklysmos

The Festival of the Flood is three days of fairs and water-throwing contests recalling Noah's Ark and the 40 days of the Great Flood.

JUNE

Lefkosia International Arts Festival

A two-week programme of art exhibitions, theatre, music and dance. It takes place in June at various venues in the city, particularly the Famagusta Gate Cultural Centre.

Lemesos International Art Festival

For ten days in June and July, the city's Municipal Gardens is the venue for a programme of music, song and dance by international and local artists.

JULY

Summer cultural events

Music, theatre, dance in Lemesos, Larnaka, Lefkosia, Agia Napa.

AUGUST

Village festivals

August and September are popular months for these (check with tourist offices for dates and locations).

SEPTEMBER

Lemesos Wine Festival

At this wildly popular festival, the city's Municipal Gardens are packed with throngs of people filling plastic cups with free wine as fast as the island's many wineries can supply it. There are also fairground stalls, folk dancing, amusements and food.

DECEMBER

Christmas

The 25th is celebrated in church followed by a family meal at home. Olive twigs and branches, symbols of purity, are placed over doorways and inside houses as decoration, while the Christmas tree symbolises life and prosperity.

Latsi, sunset

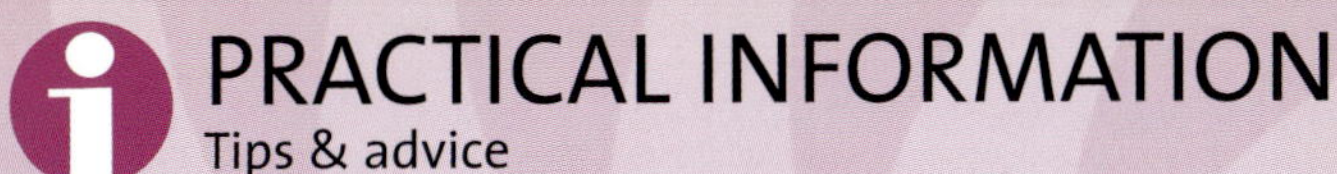

PRACTICAL INFORMATION

Tips & advice

Accommodation

Price ratings are based on a double room for one night.
£ = up to €100   **££** = €100–150   **£££** = over €150

AGIA NAPA

Bellini Bungalows £ Family run and a short walk from Sandy Bay, the harbour and lively resort centre. Choose from studios or one-bedroom apartments. ⓐ Nissi Avenue ⓣ 23 72 35 00

Nissiana Hotel ££ Situated across the road from the glorious sands and turquoise waters of Nissi Bay. Nightly entertainment and amusements for children. ⓐ Nissi Avenue ⓣ 23 72 58 00 ⓦ www.nissianahotel.com

CORAL BAY

Coral Beach £££ A popular seafront hotel offering every amenity possible – spa, craft workshop, watersports and children's club. Upgraded rooms have their own lounge serving snacks and aperitifs. ⓐ Coral Bay ⓣ 26 88 10 00 ⓦ www.leptoscalypso.com

Thalassa £££ Ultimate boutique luxury – your own butler will organise everything from airport pick-ups to excursions. Plus there's a luxury spa, great restaurants and wonderful views. ⓐ Coral Bay ⓣ 26 88 15 00 ⓦ www.thalassa.com.cy

LARNAKA

Palm Beach Hotel & Bungalows ££–£££ A stone's throw from the beach, with indoor and outdoor swimming pools, gym, tennis and squash courts and health club. The spacious bungalows have their own shared pool. ⓐ Larnaka–Dekeleia road ⓣ 24 84 66 00 ⓦ www.palmbeachhotel.com

LEMESOS

Londa £££ A chic, Italian-designed beachfront boutique hotel offering luxurious rooms and spa and top-notch cuisine. At night, the lively cocktail bar is the place to be seen. Georgiou A' Street 25 86 55 55 www.columbia-hotels.com

PAFOS

Louis Phaethon Beach ££ Plenty to amuse all the family, with children's clubs, sports facilities and regular entertainment. Family rooms are available. Aphrodite Avenue, Geroskipou 26 96 46 00 www.louishotels.com

PISSOURI/APHRODITE HILLS

Columbia Beach Hotel ££ Occupying a fabulous position on the beach of this picturesque bay, this hotel offers a relaxing escape and large swimming pool. Family rooms are available. Pissouri Bay 25 83 33 33 www.columbia-hotels.com

Intercontinental Aphrodite Hills Resort Hotel £££ Enjoy sumptuous accommodation and fine cuisine at the island's only golf resort. The Graeco-Roman spa provides the ultimate extravagance. Aphrodite Hills, near Kouklia 26 82 80 00 www.aphroditehills.com

POLIS

Natura Beach Hotel ££ Uninterrupted views of the Akamas coastline, this peaceful retreat in olive groves and orchards is a 15-minute walk from the resort centre. Chr. Papanikopoulou Street 26 32 31 11 www.natura.com.cy

PROTARAS

Silver Sands Hotel ££ On a golden sandy beach with views of beautiful Fig Tree Bay, it's a short stroll to lively restaurants and bars. Children's play areas and nightly entertainment. Demokritos Street 23 83 15 90 www.tsokkos.com

Preparing to go

GETTING THERE

The cheapest way to get to Cyprus is to book a package holiday, flight or accommodation with a tour operator or via the web. You should also check the travel supplements of the weekend newspapers, such as the *Sunday Telegraph* and the *Sunday Times*. They often carry adverts for inexpensive flights, as well as classified adverts for privately owned villas and apartments to rent in most popular holiday destinations.

If your travelling times are flexible, and if you can avoid the school holidays, you can also find some very cheap last-minute deals on the internet.

By air

There are numerous charter companies offering flights to Cyprus throughout the year. Scheduled flights from the UK are offered by the following airlines:

British Airways ⓣ 0870 850 9850 ⓦ www.ba.com
Cyprus Airways ⓣ 020 8359 1333 ⓦ www.cyprus-air.com.cy
Flyglobespan ⓣ 0871 271 0415 ⓦ www.flyglobespan.com
Monarch ⓣ 0870 040 5040 ⓦ www.flymonarch.com

Many people are aware that air travel emits CO_2, which contributes to climate change. You may be interested in the possibility of lessening the environmental impact of your flight through the charity Climate Care, which offsets your CO_2 by funding environmental projects around the world. Visit ⓦ www.climatecare.org

TOURISM AUTHORITY

Further information about Cyprus can be obtained from the **Cyprus Tourism Organisation (CTO)**. Once you reach Cyprus, you will also find CTO offices located all over the island where you can obtain local maps and information. **CTO** ⓐ 17 Hanover Street, London W1S 1YP

t 020 7569 8800 f 020 7499 4935 w www.visitcyprus.com
e informationcto@btconnect.com

Lefkosia
a 11 Aristokyprou, Laiki Geitonia (east of Plateia Eleftherias)
t 22 67 42 64

Lemesos
a 115A Spyrou Araouzou t 25 36 27 56

Pafos
a 63A Poseidonos t 26 93 05 21

BEFORE YOU LEAVE

Holidays should be about fun and relaxation, so avoid last-minute panics and stress by making your preparations well in advance.

It is not necessary to have inoculations to travel in Europe, but you should make sure you and your family are up to date with the basics, such as tetanus. It is a good idea to pack a small first-aid kit to carry with you, containing plasters, antiseptic cream, travel sickness pills, insect repellent and/or bite relief cream, antihistamine tablets, upset stomach remedies and painkillers. Sun lotion can be more expensive in Cyprus, so it is worth taking a good selection, especially of the higher factor lotions if you have children with you – and don't forget after-sun cream as well. If you are taking prescription medicines, ensure that you take enough for the duration of your visit – you may find it impossible to obtain the same medicines in Cyprus. It is also worth having a dental check-up before you go.

ENTRY FORMALITIES

No visas are required for entry into Cyprus by nations of most European countries. Nationals of other countries should contact the nearest Consulate of the Republic of Cyprus, or, if none, the nearest British Consulate. The sale of duty-free goods to EU citizens was abolished when Cyprus became a member of the EU. Visitors arriving from countries outside the EU can import the following into Cyprus:

200 cigarettes or cigars
1 litre spirits
50 g perfume
goods worth up to 175 euros.

MONEY

You will need some currency before you go, especially if your flight gets you to your destination at the weekend or late in the day after the banks have closed. Traveller's cheques are the safest way to carry money because the money will be refunded if the cheques are lost or stolen. To buy traveller's cheques or exchange money at a bank, you may need to give up to a week's notice, depending on the quantity of foreign currency you require.

You can exchange money at the airport before you depart. You should also make sure that your credit, charge and debit cards are up to date – you do not want them to expire mid holiday – and that your credit limit is sufficient to allow you to make those holiday purchases.

Don't forget, too, to check your PIN numbers in case you haven't used them for a while – you may want to draw money from cash dispensers while you are away. Ring your bank or card company and they will help you out.

Currency

The unit of currency is the euro, which replaced the Cyprus pound in January 2008. The banking system is modern, and transactions can be negotiated in all leading currencies.

There are no restrictions on the amount of foreign currency imported into Cyprus, although amounts in excess of the equivalent of US$1,000 should be declared on arrival to customs – you can then re-export it when you leave. Credit cards are widely accepted wherever tourist facilities are found.

CLIMATE

Average summer temperatures range from 21°C to 37°C (70–98°F) in the Central Plain, and from 15°C to 27°C (59–80°F) in the Troodos Mountains. Winters are mild by northern European standards, and temperatures range from 5°C to 17°C (40–60°F) in the Central Plain and from freezing to 9°C (50°F) in the mountains.

BAGGAGE ALLOWANCE

Baggage allowances vary according to the airline, destination and class of travel, but 20 kg (44 lb) per person is the norm for luggage that is carried in the hold (it usually tells you what the weight limit is on your ticket). You are also allowed one item of cabin baggage weighing no more than 5 kg (11 lb), and measuring no more than 46 by 30 by 23 cm (18 by 12 by 9 in).

In addition, you can usually carry your purchases, umbrella, handbag, coat, camera, etc, as hand baggage. Large items – surfboards, golf clubs, collapsible wheelchairs and pushchairs – are sometimes charged as extras and it is a good idea to let the airline know in advance that you want to bring these.

During your stay

AIRPORTS

Cyprus has two international airports: Larnaka is served by charter and scheduled flights, while Pafos is mainly a charter airport. Flight information is available 24 hours a day, 7 days a week for Larnaka and Pafos International Airports by ringing ⓣ 77 77 88 33.

CONSULATE

Numbers of all the major consulates on the island can be obtained through directory inquiries on 192.

ⓐ British High Commission, Alexander Pallis Street 1587, Nicosia ⓣ +357 22 86 11 00 ⓦ www.britishhighcommission.gov.uk/cyprus

COMMUNICATIONS

Telephones

Cyprus Telecommunications Authority (CYTA) public phone boxes are used increasingly rarely these days and unfortunately are often out of order. The majority take phonecards that can be purchased from kiosks and other stores. You can buy pay-as-you-go cards that can be used with most foreign mobile phones for use in Cyprus and abroad. In 2002, Cyprus changed its national telephone numbers from six digits to eight digits. All old six-digit numbers are now preceded by two-digit numbers according to their area, even when calling from within the same district. The main prefixes are: Lefkosia 22, Agia Napa 23, Larnaka 24, Lemesos 25 and Pafos 26.

Post offices

These are open from Monday to Friday, with a limited two-hour service on Saturday mornings. Post offices are closed on Wednesday afternoons, and on other afternoons there is a two-hour service. As opening times fluctuate, it is best to check with your hotel or tour operator. Every letter or card sent from Cyprus requires an extra stamp in addition to the main one – this is a one-cent Refugee Stamp. This stamp raises funds and highlights the cause of the Greek

Cypriot refugees created by the Turkish invasion of Cyprus in 1974. Blue folding Aerogrammes are also available but still require the extra Refugee Stamp.

DRESS CODES

Visitors should dress respectfully when visiting buildings of religious significance and avoid wearing shorts and sleeveless garments there.

ELECTRICITY

The electricity supply in Cyprus is 220/240 V AC (50 hertz). Electric plugs are 3-pin. If you are considering buying electrical appliances to take home, always check first that they will work in your country.

EMERGENCY TELEPHONE NUMBERS

- Police 112
- Ambulance 112
- Fire 112

GETTING AROUND

Car hire and driving Driving is on the left, and a national or international driving licence is required. Hire cars are widely available, with the price depending on model and engine capacity. The standard of driving in Cyprus is rather erratic and you should drive with caution.

In case of a breakdown, emergency telephones are located at the side of the major highways. Failing that, the locals are generally happy to help out in whatever way they can.

All of the main towns and villages in Cyprus are well served by petrol stations, but if you are heading further afield it is advisable to fill up beforehand. Petrol stations are open from 06.00 to 19.00 in summer and 06.00 to 18.00 in winter on weekdays. They close at 15.00 on Saturdays. On Sundays they are closed all day. In Lefkosia they close at 14.00 on Wednesday, while in the other main towns they are closed on Tuesday afternoons. However, almost all stations have Bank Note Acceptors (BNAs), so in practice you should never run dry.

Public transport The bus service between major towns and tourist areas is fairly good during summer – less so during the winter. There is a standard fare, regardless of how far you travel.
Taxis Within the main towns, these are metered, but tipping is expected. 'Service' taxis operate regularly between the main towns: these are a cheap and easy way to get around.

HEALTH, SAFETY & CRIME

Health hazards The heat is the biggest potential danger to your health. Dress in light clothes and try to avoid over-exposure to the sun. Wear a suitable sun lotion and ensure that you consume plenty of liquids (preferably not alcohol) and wear a hat. Remember that the danger of sunburn increases near water.
Insurance Have you got sufficient cover for your holiday? Check that your policy covers you adequately for loss of possessions and valuables, for activities you might want to try – such as scuba diving, horse riding or watersports – and for emergency medical and dental treatment, including flights home if required.

The European Health Insurance Card (EHIC) allows UK visitors access to reduced-cost and sometimes free state-provided medical treatment in the EEA, which includes EU Cyprus (south). This card is normally valid for three to five years. For further information, ring EHIC enquiries line: ⓣ 0845 605 0707. To apply for a card, ring ⓣ 0845 606 2030, pick up an application at the Post Office or visit ⓦ www.ehic.org.uk to apply online. It is possible to apply for a card on behalf of your spouse or partner, and for children up to the age of 16, or 19 if they are in full-time education.
Pharmacies on the island are operated by highly qualified staff and are well stocked, with prices generally lower than in the UK. For details of pharmacies on night duty, telephone ⓣ 192. Details of night pharmacies are also in the *Cyprus Weekly* newspaper.

Emergency treatment is available at local hospitals, but tourists should expect to pay for any treatment they receive. The standard of medical care in Cyprus is high and there are many private clinics offering high-quality and relatively inexpensive treatment. The emergency telephone number is ⓣ 112 for fire, ambulance or police – all operators speak English.

Water Cyprus's tap water is safe to drink and mostly tastes good. Many people also drink bottled mineral water. Because of several years of drought, water is in short supply, and supplies may be interrupted on occasions. Water should not be used wastefully.

Safety & crime Crime levels are low in Cyprus, but you should still take sensible precautions. Lock your car when you have parked and never leave valuables unattended. While the local police are fairly easy-going thanks to the island's low crime rate, reports of theft will be treated seriously. If you should need to report a crime or incident, inform the police immediately and provide them with as many details as possible. Check that they write down the exact information you give them. Keep a note of the date you make your statement and the name and direct telephone number of the officer who takes it, as this will be the only reference available for your case.

MEDIA

Three English-language newspapers are published on the island: the daily *Cyprus Mail* (except Mondays), the *Cyprus Weekly* (every Friday) and the *Financial Mirror* (every Wednesday).

Local television programmes are in Greek, although a wide variety of imported programming in English is also screened (with Greek subtitles). There are daily news bulletins in English on both Cyprus television and radio (details in the local press). BFBS (the British Forces Broadcasting Service) also transmits radio programmes in English all over the island.

OPENING HOURS

Shopping and business hours in Cyprus depend on the time of year. Around Greek Orthodox Easter, most places are closed for several days. In the hotter summer months, some premises close for three hours after lunch because of the heat – and because of the Mediterranean custom of having a siesta. Hairdressing salons are closed all day Thursday, but are open all day Saturday.

Shops Summer hours: 08.00–14.00, 17.00–20.00, except Wed 08.00–14.00, Sat 08.00–17.00. These are schedules set by law. Shops can close earlier: for example, this is the case for Lefkosia on Saturdays. However, they cannot open earlier. In winter, they open earlier and close earlier in the afternoon.

Tombs of the Kings, Pafos (see page 56)

Banks Normal banking hours for the public are: summer 08.15–13.00 Monday to Friday and in winter also 15.15–16.45 every Monday afternoon. Afternoon facilities for tourists are available at some branches.

RELIGION

Greek Orthodoxy is the main religion in Cyprus, and Easter is the most important event on the Orthodox calendar. Other denominations hold regular services on the island as well. These are:

Anglican

St Paul's Cathedral, Leoforos Vyronos, Lefkosia ⓣ 22 67 78 97
St Helena's, Leoforos Gr. Afxentiou, Larnaka ⓣ 24 65 13 27
Agia Napa Monastery, Agia Napa (English services) ⓣ 24 64 28 58
St Barnabas Church, Archiepiskopou Leontiou, Lemesos ⓣ 25 36 27 13

Roman Catholic

Holy Cross Church, Pyli Pafou, Lefkosia ⓣ 22 66 21 32
St Catherine's Church, 28 Oktovriou, Lemesos ⓣ 25 36 29 46
Santa Maria Church, Terra Santa Street, Larnaka ⓣ 24 64 28 58

Others

Saint Maron Maronite Church, Anthoupolis, Lefkosia ⓣ 99 68 69 38
Evangelical Church of Cyprus, Larnaka ⓣ 24 62 59 27
Armenian Church, Vasili Michailidi, Lefkosia ⓣ 24 65 44 35

TIME DIFFERENCES

Local time is two hours ahead of Greenwich Mean Time, except during Cyprus summer time, when it is GMT+3. Cyprus summer time begins on the last Sunday of March and ends on the last Sunday of October.

TIPPING

Not obligatory, but always welcome! The Cyprus Tourism Organisation (CTO) specifies a ten per cent service charge on all hotel and restaurant bills. Restaurants are required by law to display their charges.

TOILETS

Public toilets are found in bus stations and main squares. Marginally cleaner facilities are found in bars, but you should buy a drink if you are using them. Used toilet paper is placed in a waste bin alongside the toilet, not flushed down the loo.

TRAVELLERS WITH DISABILITIES

Most resorts are reasonably flat and offer wheelchair access and special parking bays. In Lefkosia, a number of roads and entertainment venues have ramps. The use of international stickers for the disabled is legally enforced in Cyprus and they can be obtained from the **Pancyprian Organisation for Disabled Persons** in Lefkosia (ⓐ PO Box 28627, CY 2081 ⓣ 22 42 63 01 ⓕ 22 31 32 50).

Generally, hotels have good facilities for people with special needs. Details for individual hotels can be found in the Cyprus Tourism Organisation's *Guide to Hotels*, travel agencies and other tourism establishments.

Larnarka and Pafos International Airports have wheelchairs, modified washrooms and truck-lifts to help disabled travellers embark and disembark from aircraft. See ⓦ http://cyprus.angloinfo.com/information/10.disabled.asp